Winter Sports in the West

Edited by

ELISE A. CORBET
The Historical Society of Alberta

ANTHONY W. RASPORICH
Department of History
The University of Calgary

Published by
THE HISTORICAL SOCIETY OF ALBERTA

c19—

CANADIAN CATALOGUING IN PUBLICATION DATA

Main entry under title: Winter Sports in the West

Includes bibliographical references
ISBN 0-929123-01-8

1. Sports — Canada, Western — History. 2. Leisure — Canada, Western —
History. I. Corbet, Elise A. II. Rasporich, Anthony W. III. Historical Society
of Alberta.

GV840.7.C3W46 1990 796.9'097124 C89-090462-6

Published by The Historical Society of Alberta
Cover design by Cliff Kadatz, University of Calgary Graphics
Printed by Hignell Printing, Winnipeg, Manitoba

Price: $11.95
Available from The Historical Society of Alberta
Box 4035, Station "C"
Calgary, Alberta T2T 5M9

TABLE OF CONTENTS

LIST OF CONTRIBUTORS

1. Greg Thomas, Head, Historic Park Planning, Prairie and Northern Region, Canadian Parks Service, Winnipeg

2. Fraser Pakes, Director of Education, Stoney Indian Tribe, Morley, Alberta

3. Donald Wetherell, Historical Resource Consultant, Edmonton

4. Carl Betke, Chief of Research, Historic Sites Service, Alberta Culture and Multiculturalism

5. Elaine Chalus, M.A. Student in History, University of Alberta

6. William B. Yeo, Chief of Historical and Archaeological Research, Western Region, Canadian Parks Service, Calgary

7. Jorgen Dahlie, Professor Emeritus, Faculty of Education, University of British Columbia

8. Gerald Redmond, Department of Physical Education and Sports Studies, University of Alberta

9. Doreen Ryan, Former Head of Athlete's Village at the Calgary Winter Olympics, 1988

10. Morris Mott, Professor of History, Brandon University

ACKNOWLEDGEMENTS

The Historical Society of Alberta had two reasons for celebration in 1987. Firstly it was eighty years old, having been incorporated by an act of the new Alberta legislature in 1907. And secondly, along with many Albertans, its members were eagerly anticipating the Winter Olympics, which were hosted by Calgary in February, 1988. They wanted to play a part in this unique experience and what better way than to take a look back at the history of winter sports in western Canada. Fortuitously they found a willing partner in this enterprise, the History Department of The University of Calgary.

All those who have organized a conference know that it takes a lot of effort, by a lot of people, as well as a lot of money. We were very fortunate to receive financial assistance from the Special Projects Fund of The University of Calgary, and as well as the provincial historical society, all three chapters of the society contributed as well: the Amisk Waskahegan Chapter in Edmonton, Chinook Country Chapter in Calgary, and the Lethbridge Historical Society. Additional funding came from K-Bro Linen Systems in Edmonton and Molson Alberta Breweries Ltd. in Calgary. We extend sincere thanks to these contributors.

We would also like to thank those members of the History Department and the Society who contributed their time to the planning and running of the conference, particularly Fred Holberton, who so ably took charge of the registration, and Bruce Ibsen, who made all the arrangements with the Edmonton Grads. Those who acted as chairmen of the sessions included Raymond Huel, Gretchen Ghent, Howard Palmer, Bruce Kidd, David Marshall, Joan Ryan, and Jean Leiper; and we extend our thanks to them as well. We also extend our thanks to Joey Dyrholm for her careful preparation of this volume for publication.

This was the second occasion on which the History Department of The University of Calgary and the Historical Society of Alberta collaborated in sponsoring a conference. In 1975 the occasion was Calgary's centennial and the proceedings were published under the title: *Frontier Calgary.* Both conferences were successful and rewarding. We can only look forward to a third.

E.A. Corbet
A.W. Rasporich

INTRODUCTION

This set of conference papers is the result of a fortuitous meeting between the two editors of this volume in the foyer of The University of Calgary Library in the fall of 1986. We speculated on the subject of conferences dealing with western Canada's history, and the conversation naturally drifted to the oncoming Winter Olympic Games in 1988. And just as serendipitously came the idea of a western Canadian history conference on the theme of winter sports in western Canada, past, present and future. The seed of an idea was planted with the two sponsoring organizations — the History Department at The University of Calgary and the Historical Society of Alberta. Further nurturing of the project occurred during 1987 when both the University Special Projects Fund and the Historical Society made funds available to support the conference slated for November of 1987.

As with all such events, a good deal of planning and supplicating of speakers was necessary to cast the formal programme which was in place by June of 1987. The conference quickly took shape and was held at the University on November 13-14, in the mood of rising excitement which by then had infected most Calgarians. The subject itself attracted a truly inter-disciplinary audience of winter sports aficionados, historical specialists (both social historians and sport historians), anthropologists and sociologists and former participants in the various sports themselves — skaters, curlers, skiers and basketball players. In the latter category, several alumni of the long-standing Edmonton Grads teams of the 1920's and 1930's attended many of the various sessions in the two-day conference. Confronted by such a formidable cast of observer-participants, those who had agreed to deliver papers at the conference knew that their contributions would receive careful scrutiny.

The keynote session was launched by Gretchen Ghent of the University Library, herself a former Olympic-level swimmer, who introduced the keynote speaker, Dr. Jean Leiper of the Faculty of Physical Education and an Olympic historian. Having received the assignment of Colour Commentator at the Olympic torchlighting ceremonies in Greece on television, Dr. Leiper was full of pre-games enthusiasm. Her talk focussed on western Canadians who had participated in the Winter Olympic Games since their inception in Stockholm in 1928 (the 1924 games were retroactively declared the first). She detailed the difficulties of identifying western Canadian contributions *per se* to various winter sports, but did relate several salient points of record. The Winnipeg Falcons were the first hockey team to score a first in the *summer* games of 1920 at Antwerp, winning by a margin of 28-1! Subsequently, the first speed skater to compete for Canada was Charles Gorman at Chamonix, France in 1924 along with our first female figure-skating competitor, Cecil Smith, at the same games. Significant break-throughs occurred in the 1932 Winter Games at Lake Placid when four Canadian men won medals in speed skating, led by Frank Stack of Winnipeg in the 10,000 meters — who competed thereafter in six successive games until 1952! Dr. Leiper then took the audience through the more impressive achievements of Canadian women in both the skiing and figure-skating events, capped by the magnificent performances by Nancy Greene of Rossland, B.C. in the 1964 and 1968 Games. More recent western Canadian performances by downhill skiers such as Calgarians Ken Read and Jim Hunter, and the cross-country marvels, the Firth sisters of Aklavik, were included in the catalogue of western Canadian achievements. Lamentably, as she pointed out, Canadian achievements at the Olympics in our premier sport of ice-hockey have not been great because the amateur-professional distinctions favoured eastern bloc countries. But, as she noted, the Winnipeg Falcons dominated in the early Games winning both in 1920 and 1932, and in 1952 the Edmonton Mercuries won the last gold medal before Soviet dominance of the sport began.

Among the other papers and presentations which are *not* recorded in this present collection of papers were several which deserve mention. The first of these was a panel following Dr. Leiper's keynote address, composed of former Alberta figure-skaters, Shirley Boyce and Laurie Brownly who were then co-chairpersons of both Skate Canada and the 1988 Winter Olympics. Both elaborated on the history of figure-skating in Alberta and Canada, setting the stage for a fine participant-observer account of speedskating given by Doreen Ryan which *is* included in this collection.

Three other notable contributions from the male side of the winter sports ledger which are not included here were those on ice-hockey, curling, and the Northwest Mounted Police. The author of *Alberta on Ice*, Gary Zeman, commented in a session on ice-hockey in Alberta, that the lack of artificial ice inhibited the development of professional ice-hockey in western Canada from the nineteen-twenties forward until the postwar era. Other negative findings were related by historian Dr. Roderick McLeod of the University of Alberta, whose research showed that the Mounties displayed a relative lack of involvement in winter sport and leisure activities, (a) because of the relative predominance of summer sports such as cricket and soccer and (b) the lack of official sponsorship for the organization of sports in the Mounted Police. This lack of organization distinguished them from the early military regiments in the West, which were more active in every facet of organized sport, both in summer and winter. Lastly, Dr. Paul Voisey, also of the University of Alberta, and author of a widely-acclaimed book entitled *Vulcan: The Making of a Prairie Community*, related in his unpublished address, the vagaries of curling as a minor activity in the early years of Vulcan's existence, compared with baseball and hockey. But with the construction of an indoor curling rink in 1922, which received a ninety-one percent support from the voting ratepayers of Vulcan, curling quickly took off, and became the premier winter sport of this prairie town. Popular among both men and women, curling was an ideal medium as the Vulcan newspaper editorialized in 1910: "From a social point of view, curling provides a mixing place that cannot be equalled." Indeed, it became the archetypal western sport, as one observer, Dr. David Jones of The University of Calgary observed. Curling, he said, imitated farming in the harsh prairie environment — hail, drought, bankruptcy, and depression — and deserved the sobriquet "shaft" rather than "curling," since farmers were shafted in sport as in life! The religious overtones inherent in the cultural sub-text of the game (heaven versus hell) have of course been explored further in that western dramatic classic by W. O. Mitchell, *The Black Bonspiel of Willie McCrimmon*.

A last but memorable event in the conference proceedings not published here was the banquet which concluded the proceedings. Its prime focus was on the "Edmonton Grads" basketball team which had several representatives in attendance, notably Betty Bowen, who commented on the team's extraordinary win-loss record of over five hundred victories versus only ten or so defeats over their entire twenty-five years of competition from 1915 to 1939. The banquet proceedings also featured an Alberta premier showing of the National Film Board's "Shooting Stars" on the subject of that famous franchise, commented on by its producers, Alan Stein and Mary McLean. This was followed by an insightful commentary on how this team's extraordinary success fit into the mainstream of Canadian women's history by sports historian and former Olympic track athlete, Dr. Bruce Kidd of the University of Toronto.

The remaining papers presented here represent the core of the printed papers delivered to the conference, proceeding from the earliest manifestation of sport and leisure activities on the western frontier, from the native peoples and fur traders to the most structured of urban sports in the west. From the plains to the mountains, from the small town to urban metropolis, the varied leisure activities of western Canadians are described here in these ten contributions to broaden our understanding of western Canadians' pursuit of leisure, pleasure and sport.

The first of these papers is by Greg Thomas, Head of Historic Park Planning in the Canadian Parks Service, Winnipeg, on the subject, "Sports and Leisure in the Nineteenth Century Fur Trade." Thomas discusses the leisure and recreational activities of the fur trade society in this article, concentrating particularly on those pursued in the wintertime, and traces the parallels between sports and recreation in Britain and the northwest. As well, he looks at the traditional games played by the native populations, who played such a dominant role in the fur trade. There is documentary evidence of a number of activities pursued by the fur traders despite a lack of facilities and extremes of temperatures. Football seems to have been one of the earliest games played by fur traders, while other sports included contests of strength and other skills, boat races, horse racing, skating and winter hunting.

A complementary paper on the native peoples' winter activities is presented by Fraser Pakes, an anthropologist, formerly an ethnologist with the Nakoda Institute at Morley, Alberta, near Calgary. His paper, '"Skill to Do Comes of Doing.' Purpose in Traditional Indian Winter Games and Pastimes," develops the theme of the title that most games played by Indian boys and girls provided training for the activities and life style of their adult years. Concentrating on winter activities, Pakes introduces us first to the hardship of winter on the prairies and the stoicism with which the native Indians adapted to this harsh climate. He then goes on to describe the games of the children, the equipment they used and the relationship they bore to future activities. At a time when inter-tribal warfare was a common occurrence, many of the children's games — and indeed the gambling activities of their elders as well — bore a direct relationship to the attitudes and skills necessary for success in battle.

The next paper specially commissioned for this collection of papers is authored by Dr. Donald Wetherell, who is an historical resource consultant in Edmonton. He has recently co-authored a book with Irene Kmet entitled *Useful Pleasures: The Shaping of Leisure in Alberta, 1896-1945*, co-published by Alberta Culture and Multiculturalism and the Canadian Plains Research Center in Regina and soon to be released in 1990. In his article, "A Season of Mixed Blessings: Winter and Leisure in Alberta Before World War II," Wetherell explores the significance of winter to the largely rural society on the prairies in the years before World War II. He outlines the activities available to the various social, economic and ethnic groups, for both rural and urban populations, and men and women, as well as the changes that resulted from the technological advances of radio and the motor car. Included is the development of such outdoor sports as curling, hockey and skiing; basketball, boxing, gymnastics and other indoor sports; unorganized activities such as tobogganing and snowshoeing; as well as the great variety of indoor activities — dancing, movies, drama clubs and winter carnivals.

His paper is followed by Carl Betke's article, "Winter Sports in the Early Urban Environment of Prairie Canada." Dr. Betke is Chief of Research of the Historic Sites Service, Alberta Culture and Multiculturalism, in which role his research interests have been multifarious. A special research interest has been Edmonton's urban history which has included various aspects of sports in an urban setting. In this article Betke explores the history of winter sports and recreational activities from several angles. Against a thematic background of social and community development, he analyses the develop-

ment of sporting activities in western prairie cities from the period 1880 to
1930, tracing their organization into leagues, commercial and promotional
ventures, the advent of artificial ice and indoor rinks and arenas, the beginnings of professionalism, and intercity contests. The article deals with most
activities which helped our pioneers survive the long prairie winters, from
hockey and curling, to basketball and badminton, as well as pool and
billiards.

The next article concentrates on just one sport in an urban community,
the famous Edmonton Grads basketball team. Elaine Chalus' article "The
Edmonton Commercial Graduates" won the annual award of the Amisk
Waskahegan Chapter of the Historical Society of Alberta in 1988. Chalus
is presently completing her master's degree in history at the University of
Alberta and has an intimate knowledge of basketball as she coached a senior
boys' basketball team when she was teaching high school students. Her
article is divided into two parts: the first section presents a factual account
of this fantastically successful basketball team: how they got started, the
coach and his methods of coaching, their growing popularity in their community and their many accomplishments. The second section explores the
experiences of the Grads from both a feminist and an integrationist historical approach. She shows the attitudes of society toward a women's highly
successful team, how the press dealt with them, and the response of the
Grads themselves and how they reacted to their success.

The next article concentrates on a much smaller centre of tourism.
"Making Banff A Year-Round Park," by William B. Yeo, Chief of Historical
and Archaeological Research for Parks Canada, Western Region, concerns
the emergence of Banff as a park for activities throughout the year and concentrates mainly on the sport of skiing over the past ninety years. It was not
until 1917, however, that yearly activities began to attract visitors to Banff
in the wintertime. That was the year of the first Banff Winter Carnival and
its famous ice palace. Curling bonspiels, snowshoe and cross country ski
races, were all part of the Carnival but its major attraction was ski-jumping.
Yeo explores this development as well as that of the various ski areas, the
technological advances in the sport and its presentation to the public. The
origins of each of the three major ski areas are analyzed, as well as the people
involved in their development, and the article concludes with current concerns about further ski development in a national park.

This article leads naturally in its discussion of skiing to Jorgen Dahlie's
paper, "Skiing for Identify and Tradition: Scandinavian Venture and Adven-
ture in the Pacific Northwest, 1900-1960." Dr. Dahlie is a specialist in multi-
cultural education and ethnic studies analysis, and is now Professor Emeritus
at the University of British Columbia and an educational consultant. Dahlie's
article looks at the activities of various Scandinavian immigrants who were
instrumental in the development of skiing and ski jumping in the Pacific
Northwest. He traces the relationship of skiing to the western mining communities, at a time when many of the Scandinavian immigrants were miners:

"mining is our bread and skiing our soul." Hegseth, Jeldness, Engen, and many others were great competitors who dominated winter exhibitions and carnivals, competitive ski racing and jumping. They attracted the interest and captured the imagination of western Canadians and fostered the development of skiing as a winter sport in the west.

This paper is followed by a discussion of what is likely Canada's most popular participant sport in winter — curling — by Dr. Gerald Redmond. Dr. Redmond is a professor in the Department of Physical Education and Sport Studies at the University of Alberta in Edmonton, and has enjoyed a long association with the history of sports. This article traces not only the development of curling in western Canada, but also this region's rising dominance in the sport since its early days in Winnipeg in the 1880's until the present time. Redmond discusses the Scottish background of the sport and gives a short introduction to the role of the Scottish settlers in Canada in this sport, in golf, and in various entrepreneurial ventures. He traces the development of the sport westward from Winnipeg, which virtually coincided with the settlement of the prairies, the advent of the bonspiels and their prizes, and women's participation in the sport.

Somewhat lesser known in the hierarchy of winter sports is that of speed-skating, the subject of the next article — a reminiscence by Doreen Ryan. Since she started speedskating in 1945, Ryan won fourteen Canadian championships and participated in two Olympic Games, in 1960 and 1964. She is a member of the City of Edmonton Sports Hall of Fame, the Alberta Sports Hall of Fame, and the Canadian Speedskating Hall of Fame. In her article, Ryan traces the development of the sport from its beginnings in the mid-nineteenth century to the present time. She grew up in Edmonton and recalls the role of skating in winter social activities. Included in the article is a discussion of the types of rinks available, as well as the development of the sport in terms of tracks, skates, clothing, coaching and financing.

The final paper, by Morris Mott, deals with Canada's premier national sport and is entitled: "The Problems of Professionalism: The Manitoba Amateur Athletic Association and the Fight Against Pro Hockey, 1904-1911." Dr. Mott, who now teaches history at Brandon University in Manitoba, played hockey for about fifteen years. He was on the Canadian National team in the late sixties and played with the California Seals in the seventies. Both teams, he ruefully admits, are now defunct! Professional hockey was played in Manitoba from 1905 to 1909, but during the following years it gradually disappeared as the Manitoba Amateur Athletic Association determined to bring about a revival of amateur hockey. This article describes the background to the reaction against professionalism in the sport of hockey, the attitudes of those involved in the dispute, and the animosities it created. In his analysis, the author provides information about the role of sporting activities in everyday life during the early part of this century, the changing definition of an amateur, and the manner in which this conflict reflected the urban-rural animosities in the province.

These papers taken together represent a significant new contribution to our understanding of Western Canadians' leisure activities in winter. The ubiquitous effects of the harsh prairie environment are evident in the manifest attempt by Westerners to integrate it into their everyday lives. Quite unlike the current activities of Canadians which are often designed to escape, rather than live with winter — either in Arizona or Hawaii, or the West Edmonton Mall — the Western Canadians described here often exulted in their hardy outdoor pursuits. Their adaptation to northern environmental adversity with a pursuit of pleasure in the patented traditions of "the true North, strong and free," made them truly Canadian in their outlook.

SPORTS AND LEISURE IN THE NINETEENTH CENTURY FUR TRADE

Greg Thomas

York Boat brigades rushing down Lake Winnipeg to beat the autumn freeze-up. Hudson's Bay Company ships weighing anchor off York Factory for the return trip to England through the ice-flows of Hudson Strait. The Indian hunter and his family heading out for another winter season on their Mackenzie River trap line. The popular images of the Canadian fur trade remain at the forefront of the Canadian imagination, particularly during the past few years as the works of Peter Newman on the Hudson's Bay Company revived popular interest in the history of the Canadian fur trade.

Despite the books of Newman and more academic accounts of fur trade society from Arthur Ray, Jennifer Brown and Gerald Friesen, what do we really know and recognize about the fur trade community, both Native and European, when they were not in pursuit of furs or survival? More specifically, how did fur trade society in the nineteenth century perceive sport or leisure activity, and what particular activities did they pursue?

It is now a well known fact that Canadian historiography has not placed a great emphasis on sport and games, despite the emergence of Canadian social history over the past two decades. There have been very few attempts to write even general narrative histories of sport and leisure activity in Canada, let alone to place sport or leisure in any social, technological, or economic context. Most authors concede a certain recreational aspect to hunting, some mention competition between canoe brigades in breathless prose, and almost all comment unfavourably on the fur trade community's tendency to overindulge in alcohol. But rare is the historian who mentions football, fireworks or checkers among the diversions of the fur trader.[1] This article will attempt in a small way to address this imbalance by considering the recreations of fur trade society, with a special emphasis on their winter activities to meet the major theme of this collection of essays.

It is generally agreed that cultures throughout history have pursued some form of "play" activities. Indeed games, diversions and amusements of one sort or another are one of the few universal manifestations of culture. Debate arises, however, when one attempts to define "leisure," "recreation," "sport," or "games." To avoid the ongoing debate among social scientists as to the definitions of these terms, this paper will follow less precise definitions. Leisure, whatever its relationship to the industrial revolution, will be defined as that "time which lies outside the demands of work, direct social obligation and the routine activities of personal and domestic maintenance." Recreation are "those activities and interests that form the typical occupation of leisure time."[2] "Games" involve play and competition, and proceed by chance or strategy; if, however, they also require physical dexterity and activity, they are "sports."

To understand the leisure and recreational pursuits of fur trade society in the nineteenth century, it is important to be aware of developments in British society at this time. I am particularly indebted to Peter Bailey's *Leisure and Class in Victorian England: Rational Recreation and the Contest for Control, 1830-1885* for offering useful insights into the development of fur trade recreation and leisure[3] and the work of Michael Payne who has written extensively on York Factory.[4] In the pre-industrial period in England, a strong popular culture of recreation emerged which was based on the rural village and tied to the seasonal nature of work. Not only were the amusements of the common people tied to the cycle of work, they were not clearly distinguished from that labour. In nineteenth century Britain, as the old traditional village community broke down, leisure time gradually became separated from work time, and it came to be pursued in special locations, usually well away from the work-place. In what Peter Bailey calls the "new leisure world" of Victorian Britain, leisure activities became the product of individual choice or preference.[5] They were also increasingly commercialized and institutionalized. Sports, for example, came to be played under codified systems of rules, and associations were developed to draft these regulations and to see that they were followed. Many sports were turned into professional activities. In Britain this was particularly true of football where the many local variants of this sport were eventually subsumed by rugby and "association" football or soccer.

Not all of these changes influenced the recreational and leisure habits of the fur traders. Professional sports did not have any direct impact on life at fur trade posts for obvious reasons, but, in general terms, the leisure and recreational patterns of the fur trade community did evolve during the nineteenth century. Peter Bailey's "New Leisure World" of Victorian Britain was not replicated in the Canadian Northwest, but elements of it can be found.

When the Hudson's Bay Company established their posts on the Bay, they came into contact with Native cultures that had long since developed their own games and recreations. During the initial contact period there was extensive cultural transferral from Native to European culture and vice versa, but it is important to note that this was not the case in the area of leisure and recreation. Indian games, sport, music, dancing and other pastimes remained almost exclusively the cultural property of Indians until well into the nineteenth century, nor did they borrow much from the Europeans.

Robert Stewart Culin, who has produced the most comprehensive study of the games of North American Indians, suggests that playing cards and "nine mens' Morris" (a form of checkers or draughts) were among the few games borrowed by the Indians from the whites.[6] Otherwise, it was not until the late nineteenth or early twentieth centuries that North American Indians played European games or sports in any numbers.

Culin divided Indian games into two general classes, games of chance and games of dexterity.[7] The Cree, for instance, played the "moccasin" game, and a "dice" game which closely correspond to Culin's games of chance. The "moccasin" game was a sleight-of-hand guessing game in which an object was hidden in one of a number of moccasins, and then one's opponent was challenged to guess which moccasin held the object. In the dice games, small pieces of stone, brass, bone, or wood were shaken or tossed in a platter. The sides of the pieces that turned up determined the score.

Indian games of dexterity took several forms. They were fond of contests of marksmanship, using bows and arrows at first, and later on, firearms. They challenged each other to run races, usually over short distances, and held wrestling and jumping contests. The Cree, as an example, played several different types of ball games. Two were primarily male games and one female. Women played a game called "tishesvy's," which James Isham translates as "a pair of stones" or testicles.[8] Two stuffed leather balls, attached together by a thong about six to ten inches long, were tossed from person to person and caught by means of sticks thirty or more inches in length. The object of the game was to carry these balls or throw them through the opposition's goal (similar to lacrosse). As these goals could be as far as one mile apart, it produced "a fine, robust class of women." Cree men played a game that consisted of throwing a ball into the air and batting it back and forth around a ring. They also played a form of "prisoner's base" in which a ball was thrown in the air, whereupon the person who caught the ball tried to run to a designated spot before the other players could stop him.

Accounts of Indians on the plains frequently refer to the important role of horses in their leisure pursuits. Daniel Williams Harmon, an articulate trader who worked for the North West Company, has left us this colourful description of the Assiniboins at play: "The Assiniboins, as well as all the other Indians in the plains, spend much of their time about their horses, and are fond of trying their speed. Their youth, from the age of four or five to that of eighteen or twenty years, pass nearly half of their time in shooting arrows at a mark, and to render this employment more interesting, they always have something at stake...from so early and constant a practice they became, at length, the best marksmen perhaps, in the world. Many of them, at the distance of eight or ten rods, will throw an arrow with such precision, as twice out of three times, to hit a mark the size of a dollar."[9]

Some Indian games or activities did eventually become popular as sports or recreations with Euro-Americans. In time, lacrosse, canoeing, and

snowshoeing all acquired a certain popularity. Lacrosse, in fact, became the
national sport in Canada, and from the 1840s until the early twentieth
century, it was one of the most popular of Canadian sports. For the most
part, however, the fur traders in the early Canadian west did not exhibit a
predilection to turn Indian games or activities into recreations, with the
possible exception of snowshoeing, which was taken up by some Hudson's
Bay Company officers for exercise and amusement.[10]

The most frequently mentioned "sport" of the fur traders was football.
In fact, in his account of fur trade society, John McDougall called it the
"national game of the North-West."[11] Mention is made of playing football
as early as New Year's Day 1734 at a Prince of Wales Fort at Churchill,
and the games remained a frequent part of the Christmas-New Year's holiday season at the Hudson's Bay Company bayside posts throughout the
eighteenth and early nineteenth centuries. When the fur trade companies
moved further westward and northward, the Christmas football game
remained a popular activity during the annual festive season between
Christmas and New Year's. At Norway House on New Year's Day, 1860, the
senior officer of the Hudson's Bay Company recorded that the villagers from
Rossville had arrived for a "quiet" game of football.[12] As Rossville was a
predominantly Indian community founded by the Wesleyan Missionaries,
this was a case of a sport crossing cultural boundaries.

Certainly, when these football games occurred, they were spirited affairs.
Alcohol and frigid temperatures, however, could stop even the keenest
contestant as this description at York Factory for December 25, 1823 attests:

> Thermometer 30 below zero
>
> Stormy weather as has been the usual custom at this place part of
> the men and some of the gentlemen turned out to a game of foot-
> ball which was not kept up with much spirit probably from the
> severity of the weather combined with a previous too free use of
> the bottle...[13]

Usually the games were "warmly contested," as well they might be considering that on occasion prizes of substantial quantities of alcohol were
offered to the victorious side. In fact, there was a close connection between
football and drink at Hudson's Bay Company establishments, and some
commanding officers may have discouraged it as a result. In 1845 York
Factory's senior officer, James Hargrave, permitted a game of football as a
reward for the men's "moderate...use of spirits" that Christmas.[14]

It is by no means clear what rules, if any, these games were played under.
The histories of popular sport in Britain emphasize that it was not until the
late nineteenth century that football separated into its characteristic forms
of soccer and rugby with codified rules. Until the introduction of rules, there
were as many versions of football as there were towns that played it. The
only common characteristics were that it was played with some sort of ball,
and it was a violent and dangerous pursuit. In England, football games were

sometimes used as covers for anti-enclosure or other riots, in which the games were used as a means to tear down the mills or fences of the local landowners.[15]

In a description of a football game at Edmonton House, British social historian Glyndwyr Williams compared this isolated group of Orkneymen to a similar match played at Kirkwall in the Orkney's on New Year's Day. Daniel Gorrie's *Summers and Winters in the Orkneys* contains this description of a football game.[16]

> Regularly as the day (New Year's) recurs there is a gathering of the populace intent on preserving one curious and time-honoured custom from extinction. The game — which should have ended with the era of cockfighting — is virtually a trial of strength, of pushing and wrestling power between "up the street" and "down the street," the grand object of the belligerents being to propel the ball to one or the other end of town. Broad Street, where the struggle commences under the shadow of St. Magnus (the Cathedral), becomes the centre of attraction about noon-tide. Sailors and porters arrive in formidable force from the purlieus of the harbour, tradesmen gather in groups, and even hoary-headed men, feeling the old glow of combative blood in their veins, hasten to the scene of anticipated contest. At one o'clock a signal pistol-shot is fired, the ball is tossed into the air from the steps of the Old Cross, and around it, soon as it bumps on the ground, there immediately gathers from all sides a dense and surging crowd. The wrestling and struggling mass sways hither and thither, sometimes revolving like a maelstrom, and at others stationary in a grim deadlock. At intervals, the ball, as if flying for dear life, makes a spasmodic bound from the crowd; but a sudden headlong rush encloses it again, and so the struggle continues as before. For onlookers, it is exciting to observe the fierce red-hot faces of the combatants, while the only appearance of good-humour displayed is a grim smile flickering fitfully across an upturned visage...heavy knock down blows, both foul and fair, are freely given and received. The struggle seldom lasts much longer than an hour, and when the seamen and porters win the day, they place the ball, as a trophy of conquest, on the top-mast of the largest ship in the harbour.

While an equally colourful description of football in the Canadian Northwest has not come to light, the games at the fur trade posts must have been boisterous and exciting. The contests also may have acted as a useful safety-valve for social tensions. The gentlemen at Hudson Bay Company posts were not averse to using their fists and feet to maintain discipline, and company servants had little choice but to submit. When the officers joined the

football game, it gave the lowly employees a chance to get back a shot of
their own in a way which did not threaten the hierarchical structure of fur
trade society.

With the exception of those football games, the residents at Hudson's Bay
Company posts throughout the northwest were not greatly inclined toward
sports. Simple contests of strength, like arm wrestling, running and jumping, or a skill like throwing stones at a mark undoubtedly took place, but
they remained spontaneous examples of play. The other "sport" introduced
in the fur trade era from Britain was cricket, and only in the more populous
Red River settlement. In the mid 1840s the British Government sent out the
Sixth Regiment of Foot to assist the Hudson's Bay Company in suppressing
the Metis free trade movement. When this assembly of young soldiers
arrived in Red River in the fall of 1846, it became an instant challenge to
entertain them. One of the senior officers, a Captain Moody, immediately
sent away to Montreal for an order of ten cricket bats, six balls, one set of
stumps and two sets of cricket rules. Although the English garrison only
stayed at Lower and Upper Fort Garry for two years, they instilled a
familiarity for the game of cricket because nearly twenty years later, the Red
River's first newspaper, *The Nor'Wester*, included accounts of local cricket
games.

Fights were commonly mentioned in the historic accounts, but whether
or not they should be interpreted as athletic contests is unclear. It has been
suggested that during the period of competition between the Northwest
Company and the Hudson's Bay Company, the officer in charge of Canoe
Brigades kept "champion prize-fighters" in their employ, to do battle when
these brigades met.[17] After the union of the companies, these regional or
brigade champions may have sought each other out to establish wider
dominance when they arrived at York Factory or Norway House to deliver
their furs. What is more likely, however, is that virtually all the fights mentioned in fur trade records were products of the irritations of fur trade life
— drink, personal antipathy, or, before 1821, competition for furs. They
were brawls, not boxing-matches, and while the spectators derived a good
deal of entertainment from them, they probably should not be dignified by
the term "sport."

Perhaps the most enduring image of the Canadian fur trade is that of the
Nor'wester canoe or York Factory Brigade making their way along the water
routes of the interior. Marjorie Wilkins Campbell, in her book *The North-
west Company*, offers an exciting account of canoe brigades racing down
Lake Winnipeg impelled by the sheer joy of competition and collective pride.
She writes:

> The great highlight of Lake Winnipeg was a race between the
> regularly laden canoes and those going to Lake Athabasca...
> year after year...the race on Lake Winnipeg became more and
> more an event to be talked of throughout each ensuing winter...

sometimes as many as a hundred canoes raced, each brigade keeping formation...across wide, shallow, choppy Lake Winnipeg the Athabascans hurled their challenges. The others increased speed. Forty-five strokes to the minute. Fifty strokes.[18]

While there was a healthy spirit of competition between the canoe brigades, it is ludicrous to suggest that the North West Company officers would allow their men to exhaust themselves in a race so early in their travels, even if the canoemen wanted to. Far more plausible are the accounts of short boat races held at company posts as a diversion. In the summer of 1825 at York Factory a race was held between "the Govrs new boat and Montreal light canoe" with eight men in each boat.

Races by water transportation were not the only competitions enjoyed during the fur trade era. Horse racing was a big New Year's Day event, particularly in the Red River settlement where the Red and Assiniboine rivers were kept clear by prevailing north winds. On New Year's Day enthusiastic spectators lined the race course near Upper Fort Garry where Hudson's Bay Company officers and the more prosperous settlers matched their blood horses in the day's racing program, sometimes for considerable stakes. The Red River Weekly, *The Nor'Wester*, described this racing event of January 1, 1863:

> The Post Office and stores closed, all business was suspended while the learned postmaster with a bet of some pounds on his little Canadian mare "Pussy," raced her on the frozen river against a fast French steed called "Nowhere." The Horses were decorated with flowers and ribbons, the enthusiastic onlookers milled along the course and cheered, and the postmaster's little nag, a stylish beast trained in Detroit, won.[19]

Racing horses was also a popular pastime at other Hudson's Bay Company establishments such as Fort Carlton and Edmonton House.

Fur traders did occasionally engage in other physical recreations that were neither sports nor games. Some appear to have found travel between posts as much a diversion as a duty. Others took a certain pleasure in snowshoeing as both exercise and a necessary complement to winter hunting. R. M. Ballantyne's descriptions of "rambles" on snowshoes leave a strong impression of the pleasure young officers derived from this pastime, particularly the joy they derived from the accidents of beginners. In the case of snowshoeing, much of the recreational value of these activities came about as a result of their association with hunting. It was, moreover, almost inclusively a pastime of Hudson's Bay Company officers. Hudson's Bay Company servants may well have enjoyed tramping about the woods on snowshoes or carrying correspondence between posts, but for them it was simply a more enjoyable form of work than cutting wood or packing furs.

Although the fur trade era preceded the advent of hockey, they did enjoy

The old (top) and new style of sleigh driving in the Red River Territory, Manitoba

skating at the various Hudson's Bay Company establishments. Unfortunately, it only creeps into the historic records when it resulted in an accident. It may also be that few company employees engaged in it since at the time it was a fairly dangerous activity. Until the first boot skates made their appearance in the 1860s, skates were attached to the participant's own shoes by means of tight foot and ankle straps and a screw driven into the heel. Since river ice was not particularly smooth, skating on it must have been risky. James Clare in a letter to William Lake offers confirmation of the difficulties faced by skaters at York Factory.

> As to skating here it is but very poor for we only had a week or so of it in the fall of the year and that was far from being good as the ice was by no means so smooth as the polished surface of a mirror so that I enjoyed but little of it.[20]

As mentioned earlier, hunting and fishing came to be seen as recreational activities in the nineteenth century, particularly by officers of the Hudson's Bay Company. This was a particularly significant change from the eighteenth century when a good deal of the hunting for provisions was carried on by the Homeguard Indians, and fishing was considered a particularly unpleasant chore. When company employees did hunt and trap in the eighteenth century, if not for food, they were after furs as a means of supplementing income, or for personal use while in the Northwest.

In the nineteenth century at Hudson's Bay Company bayside posts, a competitive element was added to the spring goose hunt to encourage the Native hunters. At Moose and York factories, the hunter who brought in the first goose of the season was given a prize. Originally it consisted of a bottle of rum and a scarlet feather to wear as a mark of his hunting prowess, but during the 1840s the bottle of rum was discontinued, at least officially, as part of the company's campaign to discourage alcohol consumption. Instead, the lucky hunter was given "two pounds of sugar, one pint of molasses."[21]

Increasingly, at fur trade posts throughout the northwest, it came to be believed that clerks and officers required the exercise afforded by hunting to maintain their health, and that the nature of their work meant that they needed added leisure time. As early as the 1820s it became the policy of those in charge at York Factory to allow clerks to take time off from their duties to hunt as exercise.

> My days are past [sic] at the desk, from nine in the morning till eight in the evening, tho' this may be considered long hours, yet they pass over lightly. I take a turn on snowshoes for a few miles with my gun, whenever I feel inclined for a walk, besides Saturday is always a holiday so that of the week not more than five days are devoted to business.[22]

In certain important respects the games, sports and active physical recreations of the fur traders differ from those enjoyed by their fellow Britons in the nineteenth century. Sports like cricket, boxing, bowls, and to a lesser extent, horse racing, had little impact on leisure in the Canadian northwest despite their popularity in Britain and more populated areas of North America. The reasons for this are primarily practical — horses were raced at inland posts where they were available and where suitable land for horses could be found. Sports that required open or prepared fields like tennis, bowls or cricket required a large expenditure of time and money. Boxing did not develop as a sport, because it was so frequently an impromptu part of the fur trade life. Less simple to explain are the absence of the "blood sports" so popular in Britain in the eighteenth and early nineteenth centuries. Bull, bear and badger-baiting, cock and dog fighting, setting terriers on rats and a host of other unpleasant spectacles were an important part of the popular recreations of Britain. They have no direct equivalent in fur trade society, although there were not real practical impediments to such sports being developed at fur trade communities. Perhaps fur traders got enough experience hunting or trapping personally to lessen the urge to torment animals as sport.

In other ways, there are definite parallels between sports and recreation in Britain and the northwest. In both societies, recreations were often communal, as in the case of football. They made use of the resources of the community, its fields, waterways, game and so on, and they were tied to the rhythms of work. In both societies, sports and recreation were undergoing important changes. Popular recreations in Britain were under attack from middle and upper class reformers who wished to "civilize" popular sports and recreations to make them less inclined towards excesses of violence. In fur trade society this process can be seen in the attempt to make football games a reward for good behavior, not an excuse for settling scores and excessive drinking. The communal nature of popular recreations was also breaking down under the impact of hardening class lines and distinctions. Many sports and recreations, which in the past had drawn participants and supporters from across class lines, became increasingly class-bound. And it was not always the middle and upper classes that appropriated activities for themselves and excluded other classes. The working class in England in the nineteenth century essentially took over "association" football and the music hall and made them expressions of itself. There seems to be a direct parallel, however, between the tendency in fur trade society for hunting to become a prerogative of officers only, and a similar phenomenon in Britain which saw in the nineteenth century a concerted effort to limit hunts to aristocratic and upper middle class participants only.

This article has focussed upon the physical activities of the fur traders during the leisure hours. It should also be mentioned that fur trade society had its intellectual side as well; the growth of personal and company libraries as well as major enthusiasm for the field of natural history are interesting intellectual pursuits that gained popularity within the fur trade community as the nineteenth century progressed. It is also important to remember that leisure and sports were tied very closely to the celebrations and holidays of the fur traders. During the 1820-70 period, this meant something like one-third of the year would have been "time-off" for employees at Hudson's Bay Company posts. Certainly the most important holiday period at fur trade posts was celebrated between Christmas Eve and New Year's Day. But other days such as Guy Fawkes, St. George's Day (April 23rd), St. Andrew's Day and significant events during the course of the year were marked by a holiday. The highlight of these holidays was usually the evening dance which generally attracted the entire community. Music was provided by fiddlers, or in their absence any other available instruments. The dances were mostly Scottish reels at which the Indian women were not particularly accomplished, but which they enjoyed immensely. Local dances became popular if York Factory is any example, with popular names such as the Rockaway, The Curfew Lancers, the York Factory Breakdown, the Hudson Bay Jig, and the Polar Bear Walk Around.

In conclusion, if one examines the leisure pursuits of the fur trade communities scattered throughout the northwest, the picture of fur trade society that emerges is one at odds with traditional depictions of fur trade life. It was not a life of uninterrupted toil, and fur traders enjoyed a wider variety of sporting and recreational pursuits than has been generally portrayed. Nor was fur trade society static in the area of recreation and leisure. The development of fur trade leisure and recreation was primarily a reflection of the sports, recreations and pastimes of Britain, and the changes they underwent during the eighteenth and nineteenth centuries, tempered by the isolation and small scale of the Canadian fur trade community.

Christmas Ball in Bachelors' Hall

NOTES

1. See Michael Payne, "A Social History of York Factory, 1788-1870" Manuscript Report Series, Canadian Parks Service, 1984, p. 77. This paper is indebted in large part to the excellent research on York Factory and the Canadian fur trade prepared by Michael Payne.
2. See Peter Bailey, *Leisure and Class in Victorian England: Rational Recreation and the Contest for Control, 1830-1885* (London: Routledge & Kegan Paul, 1978), p. 6.
3. *Ibid.*
4. Michael Payne, *op. cit.*
5. *Ibid*, p. 78. See also R. W. Malcolmson, *Popular Recreations in English Society, 1700-1850.* (Cambridge University Press, 1973), pp. 5-14.
6. See Robert Stewart Culin, *Games of the North American Indians* (New York, AMS Press, 1973), p. 32.
7. *Ibid*, p. 31.
8. James Isham, *James Isham's Observations on Hudson's Bay, 1743* (Toronto: Champlain Society for Hudson Bay Record Society, 1949), p. 111.
9. See Daniel Williams Harman, *Sixteen Years in the Indian Country: the Journal of Daniel Williams Harmon 1880-1896* ed. W. Kaye Lamb (Toronto: Macmillan, 1957).
10. Michael Payne, *op. cit.* p. 82.
11. John McDougall, *Forest, Lake and Prairie-Twenty Years of Frontier Life in Western Canada — 1842-62* (Toronto: William Briggs, 1895), pp. 83-84.
12. Hudson's Bay Company Archives (HBCA), Norway House Post Journal, A. Series, January 1, 1860.
13. HBCA, B. 239/a/132, fo. 11, 25 Dec. 1823.
14. Michael Payne, *op. cit.*, p. 83. See also HBCA, B.239/a/163, fo 133d, 30 Dec. 1845.
15. Michael Payne, *op. cit.*, p. 83.
16. Daniel Gorrie, *Summers and Winters in the Orkneys,* (London: 1865), pp. 82-84.
17. Isaac Cowie, *The Company of Adventurers: A Narrative of Seven Years in the Service of the Hudson's Bay Company During 1867-1874,* (Toronto: William Briggs, 1913), p. 129.
18. Marjorie Wilkins Campbell, *The North West Company.*
19. Provincial Archives of Manitoba, *The Nor'Wester, January 1, 1863.*
20. Provincial Archives of Manitoba, MG 1, D11, William Lane Correspondence, James Clare to William Lane, 15 February, 1847.
21. HBCA, B. 239/a/155, fo. 40, 28 April 1842.
22. Michael Payne, *op. cit.*, p. 91.

"SKILL TO DO COMES OF DOING"
PURPOSE IN TRADITIONAL INDIAN WINTER GAMES AND PASTIMES

Fraser Pakes

This paper's title comes from a quotation in a Sioux autobiography. It signifies that for the Indian in the nineteenth century, life activities had a purpose at all times. The holistic view of life of the times had inevitable ramifications for recreation. At the same time this did not prevent the Indian from having as much fun in his society as anyone else in any other community. Joking and practical joking were as prevalent on the plains as anywhere. For the Blackfoot, Napi — Old Man — was both a creator and a trickster whose exploits were recounted with glee and much appreciation around the nightly campfires.

Let us consider for a moment the environment in which the Indian lived. The extreme continental climate experienced by those on the Plains is at least made bearable by our modern technological innovations. For the nineteenth century Indian, surviving through a particularly cold spell must have been hard indeed. While the stereotypical approach to the Plains Indian made of him some sort of super-human individual with mysterious powers of survival, the historic record does tend to show that through a rigid regime he was able to withstand and thrive within this forbidding climate.

Paul Kane in his travels across Canada related an incident where one of the Iroquois in his party slipped off a log into deep water while hauling the boat they were travelling in, which had got into shallow water. The man was rescued, but five minutes later his "clothes were stiff with ice. I asked him if he was not cold, and his reply was characteristic of the hardihood of the Iroquois...'My clothes are cold, but I am not.'"[1] In November of 1847, on his return journey, Kane crossed Jasper Lake. He noted in his journal that when the Indians came to ice or hard frozen snow, where they had to remove their snowshoes, they also took off their moccasins to preserve them. "This walking barefooted on the ice in such intense cold would seem dangerous to the inexperienced, but, in fact, the feet of those who are accustomed to it suffer less in this way than they do from the ice which always forms on the inside of the moccasin...as the ice thus formed cracks into small pieces and cuts the feet."[2]

The staple diet of the Plains Indian based as it was on the buffalo provided him with a rich diet of protein and fat. It has been estimated that the average male Indian of the nineteenth century ate close to seven to eight pounds of buffalo meat a day.

The tipi as the main dwelling of the plains Indian provided him with a functional shelter well able to withstand the rigours of winter. In earlier times the covering was made of buffalo hide, while in the latter part of the nineteenth-century canvas was invariably used. It was the tipi liner that made the difference no matter what the covering. This curtain which was attached to the tipi poles for the first five feet or so, hung around the interior walls and ensured that the cold air was separated from the warm within the tipi, and passed behind the curtain formed well away from the backs of the occupants. And buffalo robes used in quantity provided more than sufficient warmth.

These material comforts were not the whole story of the Indian's fight against the cold. The Indian was himself well inured from most cold by the rigorous training he received in youth. The younger Henry described some Peigans he observed one winter:

> They never wear mittens. I have frequently seen them come into our houses after a ten or fifteen days march over the plains, in the depth of winter, with the thermometer thirty to forty degrees below zero, dressed with only shoes, leggings, and a robe — nothing else to screen them from the cold.[3]

Charles A. Eastman said that "Our sports were molded by the life and customs of our people, indeed we practised only what we expected to do when grown."[4] Young boys were expected to toughen their bodies for the challenges they would experience as warriors and hunters. There are many traditions of boys having to break the ice of lakes and rivers and take a morning plunge in winter. Where no water was available, then they would be expected to roll in the snow. Early to bed and early to rise were the orders of the day.

Because of the practicalities of games in the lives of the Indians, very little division was shown between games played in the seasons. This was particularly so in games involving horses and bows and arrows. Horse races carried out in the summer camps were sometimes held in winter, too. Both boys and girls were able to ride by the time they were five-years old. To train them they were put in a woman's high-pommelled saddle and rawhide ropes were tied around the front and rear pommels enclosing them safely. Later these were withdrawn as the child gained confidence. Children could ride bareback or double as the need arose, all based upon real-life necessities that sometimes occurred. Unless there were severe physical or mental disabilities, it is true to say that all plains Indians could ride. Games were devised

on horseback all of which had to do with skill and maneuvering at all seasons
in warfare. This is where such actions as the 'overhang,' in which a rider
hung under the neck of his galloping horse and shot at the enemy, were
taught and practised.

While on horseherding duties, young boys would often act as though they
were going to war, and 'attack' their own camp in order to steal meat. They
would charge at the best-looking supply of meat and ride off with it, and
while the adults tried to catch them, they did not succeed. The boys would
then ride back to their stations and hold a feast.[5] Such actions as these had
obvious implications for their adult years. Boys on the Alberta plains would
be going to war probably in their early teens, sometimes as early as thirteen.
Consequently, such games soon became the real thing early in their lives.
Bodily co-ordination and the ability to make quick decisions in the middle
of battle were of obvious crucial concern in early training.

Girls were not expected to undergo the exacting discipline experienced by
the boys. From early age girls were trained for the responsibilities they would
assume while still relatively young. There is some uncertainty whether there
were toys for toys' sake. The beaded ball is of late date, and is the exception
rather than the rule. Girls more or less apprenticed to their mothers, older
sisters and other female relatives to learn the essential skills they would later
take on as wives and mothers. Dolls taught the child the culture to which
she belonged — the beadwork designs, the cut of the clothing, and their
meaning. A miniature cradleboard allowed the girl to practice the method
by which the baby was safely contained by it. A model horse was in fact a
scale model of the real thing given to her so that she could practise loading
it correctly for transportation of the family goods, with miniature replicas
of the parfleche bags and travois.

There was certainly opportunity for girls to play in groups, as with the
ball game played by teams of girls. However, the emphasis here was on
co-operation rather than competition. They learned to live together through
experiencing the tensions and potential factionalism through competition.

SPINNING TOPS
One of the "all-absorbing winter sports" was spinning tops.[6] The tops were
heart-shaped and made of wood, horn or bone. Among the Blackfoot, great
care was taken in making these tops. It was important that the wood used
be well-seasoned in order not to be too heavy. Birch was commonly used,
the bark either being left on, or removed in sections. The tops were painted
or otherwise decorated in order to identify ownership. A long thong of buckskin was used to propel them. The handle was a stick some foot long,
sometimes whittled to make it spoon-shaped at one end. From two to fifty
boys might play at any one time, and each one whipped his top until it
hummed. One then took the lead, the rest following in what was really an
obstacle course. The top had to spin all the way through, and had to cross
bars of snow in the spoon end of the whip. Sometimes the top would be

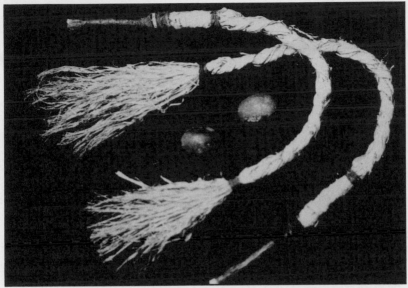

Ice stone tops and whips made of bark lashes. Credit: Glenbow Museum

tossed in the air on to another spot of ice or smooth crust from twenty to fifty paces away. The winner was the top that spun the longest.

A version common among the Indians of Alberta made use of egg-shaped pebbles and a whip with bark lashes. The players for this game were in pairs, and they sent the rocks spinning, and when at high speed drove them together. The one that stopped spinning first lost the game. If the game was played on hard snow, the players first dug a shallow trench and the tops had to cross over it while spinning. If one went into the trench, it could be whipped out or thrown out by hand. The interpretation of this game's name approximates to "knocking it."[8] Sometimes it was seen as a fighting game, the two rocks representing two different tribes. One rock would be made to 'attack' the other, and the rock knocked out of action would allow the winning boy to cry out that he had "killed a…(member of a tribe)."

In other versions of top-spinning, attempts were made to keep tops within a prescribed area, while knocking others out of it. All versions of these top games were regarded as a winter-only activity, and among the Cheyenne, for instance, there was a belief that unwanted hair would grow on the body if the game were played in summer. As soon as the ice began to break up on the lakes and rivers, tops and all other winter games' equipment were thrown into the water and carried away by the current.[9]

SNOW SNAKES

A game commonly referred to as 'snow snakes' was also common on the Alberta plains. The object of this game, usually played by women, was to see how far they could throw willow sticks across the ice. The sticks were often tipped with buffalo calves' horns, and it is said that the women used long sticks, the men, short ones.[10] This would accord with the descriptions of ribs being used by the men in some tribes.

A piece of buffalo or beef rib about seven inches long was used at one end of which two feathers much in the way an arrow was fletched. The rib was thrown down with a forward movement so that it would slide along the ice.

> If the rib happened to be quite flat, it would, when given a strong push, go up in the air, 'fly along;' if on the other hand, the rib happened to be round, it would not go up in the air like the other one, but would keep to the ice, or rather, it would go up for a few feet, then fall down, then go up in the air again, and then slide along the ice.[11]

TOBOGGANING

Tobogganing was another popular activity among young Indians, and buffalo ribs were used to construct a serviceable sled. Six or seven of the long ribs of a buffalo were separated from the backbone and reassembled in the same order. They were fastened together tightly at each end by a rawhide rope that wound across a cross piece of split willow. The seat was a piece of the leg skin of a buffalo, tied at each end to the willow cross bars and a

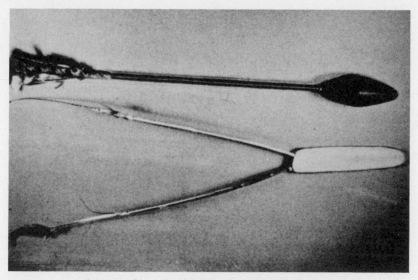

Snowsnakes. Credit: Charles Miles Collection

buffalo-tail ornament was sewn or tied to the rear of the seat. A rawhide rope, tied to the front end, served to pull the sled uphill and guide it in sliding down. The sled was prepared for use by moving it around until the runners were coated with ice.[12]

Sometimes a strip of bass-wood bark, perhaps four feet long and about six inches wide was used as an alternative to the more complex sled described above. The boy or girl stood on one end and held the other as the slippery inside of the bark was on the outside, the rider was able to coast down long hills at a fair speed.[13]

Besides simply riding downhill on such sleds, the boys often followed or chased the girls on theirs. The girls were the "buffalo," and the boys were the "hunters." When the boys caught them, they counted their "kill."

SLIDING GAMES
Making a sliding area on the ice was, of course, a common practice among all children. A boy or girl might slide alternately, and when the whole party had slid one way, they would return, sliding in the opposite direction.[14] Blackfoot boys would run and slide repeating aloud in Blackfoot — "Man its sure true" — as many times as they could before they came to a stop.[15] Actual ovals for racing were cleared on some rivers, and both boys and girls took part.[16] In deeper snow, the children played a hopping game in which the boys tried to see who could hop furthest on one leg in the snow.

RING AND PIN GAME
This game is an example of a year-round activity. A number of hollow sections of bones, about two inches in length, were strung together and a needle some eight to ten inches long was attached to one end of the string. The needle was often metal, but in earlier times was made of grease-wood or bone. The bones usually had holes bored through their sides, which counted for only one point if the needle caught them. In playing the game, the bones were swung with the needle pointing away from the body in such a way that when they were horizontal, a sudden movement backward of the needle drew them over its point. The best players could usually catch at least half the bones at a throw. Small loops of beads at the end of the string added to the permutation of scores possible. Each bone had a value of increasing value, ten, twenty, thirty, forty, etc. Sticks were used as counters, and were placed in a neutral pile to begin with, with the players drawing from the pile as many as they were entitled to in the throws. When all the pile had been divided up in this way, the players began to win sticks from each other.[17]

MEDICINE WHEEL GAME
Karl Bodmer, the Swiss artist who accompanied Prince Maximillian Zu Wied on his Missouri expedition in 1833-34, was one of the first to record the playing of the medicine wheel game. In a famous winter scene personally observed by him, two Missouri village Indians are seen playing this widely

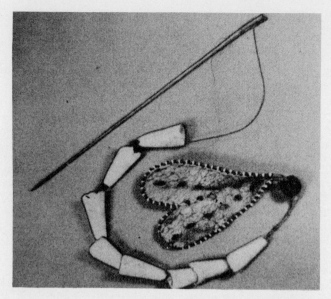

Ring and Pin Game. Pin and bones. Credit: Charles Miles Collection

understood game. Basically, a small hoop about seven centimetres in diameter, with six or seven spokes radiating from a hollow centre, was rolled by one of the players towards a log placed crosswise about six metres distant. Two players followed the hoop, and when it was about to fall flat, threw their arrows under it. The count was based upon the position of the spokes over the arrow. The spokes might have different colours such as white, black, yellow, red, symbolizing perhaps, horses. Sometimes the players would announce which spoke they were going to try for. One might say, "I captured a black horse from the Nez Perce, and so I will strike black." Often betting would be associated with the game.

This hoop and pole game definitely had hunting connotations in most of its forms. Calling the buffalo was associated with this game in the old days, and the rolling hoop represented the buffalo.

BOW AND ARROW GAMES
Many of the games played specifically by boys and men derived from the weapons used by the Plains Indians of the time. Of these the bow and arrow remained the paramount weapon for both hunting and war, and all bow and arrow games drew on the skill of the participants both in accuracy and in speed. A male relative would make the boy a miniature bow and a set of arrows to encourage him to become proficient in their use. By eight to ten

Blackfoot hoop and arrow. Credit: Denver Art Museum

years of age, a boy was able to kill small animals and birds — some of the latter on the wing.

In some games, the bow was rested in a diagonal position, while a player tapped an arrow several times on the string and then suddenly released so that it travelled several feet. The next player followed suit trying to make his arrow fly and rest on the first arrow. If no one succeeded in this, all the arrows in the first go round were put aside as stakes, and the game recommenced.[18]

Sometimes three arrows were set up in a row and the player getting his arrow closest to the middle one was the winner. As a second part to this activity the one nearest then threw up in the air a bunch of grass, that had been previously prepared and tied with buckskin. Should he hit the grass target in the air, he won again. The stakes in these games were nearly always arrows.[19]

In yet another version, an arrow was shot into a bank and became the target for all. The winner then used the grass target as above and used all the arrows previously shot at the bank by the other participants. Every time he hit the grass target, he won that arrow. The grass target was held in the bow hand and then by a swing of the arm released into the air.[20]

Sometimes a boy might tie a piece of rope to a chunk of meat and run with it, sometimes swinging the target around in circles over his head, while others shot at the moving target. Shooting arrows for a long distance was another test of capability, and here a strong bow and a powerful arm and hand were important for success.

In mock battles between boys, if a boy was hit by a blunt arrow, the others would 'doctor' him by squeezing the juice from weeds on his wound.[21] Catlin was one of the first to record such 'battles' where children under the direction of adults practised the strategies of war.

GAMES AS WAR

The close link between the games and pastimes played and the realities of aggression and warfare on the plains were more than coincidental. Within the belief and value systems of the Plains Indians was the equation of games (and for that matter gambling) equalling fighting or war.[22] We learn for instance that:

> Playing for stakes was always a favourite, and many of the games were rarely played except in gambling. Gambling is often spoken of as fighting or war, and in turn war is spoken of as gambling.[23]

The Cherokee for one used the expression that games were "the little brother of war."[24] Such a concept is reflected in at least one myth where the players' scalps were at stake.

For much of the nineteenth century the Plains Indian existed in a world where daily life was lived with the knowledge that one might very well not see the end of the day — the odds of losing one's life being so great in a region of inter-tribal strife. Second World War airmen playing baseball along the airstrips while waiting to be called into action were analogous examples of this living proximity to death. Recorders of the biographies of nineteenth century warriors' found that their informants often treated their lives as one long trail of war interspersed with virtually meaningless short intervals of peace!

Mike Mountain Horse once commented that:

> "Do we wonder now that the Indian was born a warrior? From his childhood, fighting was inculcated into his young mind. Naturally he aspired to that position in his tribe which would bring him honour as a great and noble warrior."[25]

At another level, the Indian saw and understood that gambling and war were linked by the perception that superiority had to be established as proof of a person's worth, through a form of rivalry that always involved personal risk. This risk was greatest when the natural balance between opposing forces was disturbed. The individual had to prove that his own resources were equal to those by which he was threatened: something he had to do to avoid defeat. Such defeat in either gambling or war was disastrous as the warrior's own worth was at stake. Just as he sought out the strongest foes in war, so he gambled with the man whose skill most nearly matched his own. The mythological "Twins," who represented or controlled the opposing powers — night and day, male and female — were the original patrons of play. Their games were now played by men.

All games emphasized an individual's power and ability. Although groups and societies were involved, eventually it was the individual versus the individual. War, for instance, was always a series of individual encounters. The "hand game" was warlike with players hiding bones (themselves) from the enemy. In original tales the contest was between night-and-day creatures. Each wanted perpetual night or perpetual day, but the battle has always been inconclusive so that day and night continue to alternate. In the same way, fighting between eternal enemies reached no conclusion, the essential equality of the opposing forces always ideally restoring equilibrium. Games such as these were not gifts from the white man, but came from myths and rituals of the past. A cultural hero often defeated some member of the human race in a game.

If the Battle of Waterloo was indeed won on the playing fields of Eton then we might be tempted to say that intertribal battles on the Plains were won in the play areas of the Indian camps. Elders both instructed and watched the individual children carefully, so as to sort out the ones showing the greatest promise as future warriors. In games where missiles were projected towards one another, casualties were frequent. In one recorded instance where mud balls were flung with force from willow wands, a boy had his eye knocked out. The boy took time out to return to his lodge where his father dressed the wound, gave him a pep-talk, and sent him back into the fray. Further tests of an individual's courage took place when 'captives' were taken in boys' group fights. The captors subjected the captives to much harassment, an ordeal which directly imitated real-life situations to be faced as adults. Military societies within the tribes further encouraged this type of activity. Where a system of two societies operated, there was a carefully encouraged competitive spirit nurtured between them. Raids were carried out on other societies for property, and sometimes this extended to the stealing of wives from the opposite society.[26]

Some ethnologists have seen war itself compared to a vast game on the Plains — a deadly game, but nonetheless a game. The concept of the coup with its hierarchy of honours, was avidly followed by warriors seeking recognition and fame. Trying to outdo the opposite number in daring exploits led to extraordinary feats of bravery and bravado. The large summer camps allowed for a recapitulation of the glories of the past through the medium of mock battles, while allowing continuous practice for the future.

THE ENDURING TRADITION
Today some have seen a link with the past in contemporary Indian winter sports interests. Hockey, and now rodeo, thanks to the increase in indoor rodeo centres in Alberta, are two of the favourite sports. The relationship

between rodeo and the old-time use of the horse is self evident. Hockey continues the tradition of contact sports for male Indians, and is sometimes seen as a continuation of the inter-tribal wars in the hockey tournaments between tribes. While teamwork is stressed, there is still room for the individual to shine. There is still an understanding that the individual who outshines others reflects glory back on his own people, and brings added power to the tribe as a whole.

CONCLUSION

In the nineteenth century the Plains Indian approached his recreation in the same way he approached other aspects of his daily life. There had to be an holistic approach to all he did. The simple act of throwing an arrow at a little hoop bowling along a smooth stretch of ice, for example, was more than just a game. It involved the worth of the player in relation to all others around him; it involved the sacred origins of the people themselves; and it looked forward and backward in time. Prayers accompanied nearly all recreational activities. To win, to succeed, needed more than the individual had to give. Only with his body in harmony with the forces around him, and with an understanding between him and his Creator, could he hope to accomplish victory. Today we have added layer after layer to our own perceptions of "playing the game." Yet it is only a thin veneer of civilization after all. Beneath it lie the very elemental forces and motivations that drove the Indian to pursue his own activities in the winter time.

NOTES

The quotation used in the title of this paper comes from the words of Charles A. Eastman (Ohiyesa)

1. Paul Kane, *Wanderings of an Artist Among the Indians of North America* Edmonton: Hurtig Ltd. 1968, October 11, 1846. p. 100.
2. *Ibid.* p. 244.
3. E. S. Curtis, *The North American Indian,* New York: Johnson Reprint Corporation 1980 (1928). Vol. 18, p. 180.
4. Charles A. Eastman, *Indian Boyhood* New York: Dover Publications 1971. p. 54.
5. A. L. Kroeber, *Ethnology of the Gros Ventre* New York: AMS Press 1978 (1908). p. 182.
6. Eastman, *op.cit.* p. 58.
7. *Ibid.* p. 58.
8. Clark Wissler, "The Social Life of the Blackfoot Indians" *Anthropological Papers of the American Museum of Natural History* New York 1911. Vol. VII, Part 1, p. 55.

9. George Bird Grinnell, *The Cheyenne Indians* Lincoln: University of Nebraska Press 1972. Vol 1. p. 315.
10. Kroeber, *op. cit.* p. 190.
11. Biren Bonnerjea, "Reminiscences of a Cheyenne Indian," *Society of Americanists* Vol 27. n.s. pp. 133-134.
12. John C. Ewers, *The Blackfeet* Norman: University of Oklahoma Press 1958. p. 151.
13. Eastman, *op. cit.* p. 58. A form of sled was used in the summer months when the grass was really green. Toboggans of rawhide were used on the hillsides. The front was held up and bent over and the bottom soon became very smooth. The purpose was very practical, the sliding removing the hair from the hide and thus saved the women from some of the chore associated with achieving such a state. (see for instance Kroeber, *op. cit.* p. 190).
14. Kroeber, *op. cit.* p. 190.
15. Ewers, *op. cit.* p. 153.
16. *Ibid.*
17. See for instance Kroeber, *op. cit.* p. 182-183.
18. *Ibid.* p. 187.
19. *Ibid.* p. 187-188.
20. Wissler. *op. cit.* p. 56.
21. Ewers. *op. cit.* p. 149.
22. Wissler. *op. cit.* pp 53-62.
23. *Ibid.* p. 59.
24. Sigmund A. Lavine, *The Games the Indians Played* New York: Dodd Mead and Company 1974. p. 9.
25. Mike Mountain Horse, *My People the Bloods* Calgary: Glenbow-Alberta Institute 1979. p. 13.
26. See for instance the Lumpwood and Fox society activities of the Crows described by Lowie, "Military Societies of the Crow Indians," *Anthropological Papers of the American Museum of Natural History,* Vol. XI, Pt. 1, pp 3-217.

A SEASON OF MIXED BLESSINGS:
WINTER AND LEISURE IN ALBERTA BEFORE WORLD WAR II

Donald G. Wetherell

In Canadian social history, climate is not usually judged to be a significant factor. Rather, the primary influences on society are commonly seen as class, income, urbanization and, among others, social and economic structures. With the exception of Judith Fingard's pioneering and challenging work on the meaning of winter for the poor of early Canada,[1] Canadian historians have been content to emphasize Canada's northern location in terms of nationalism, patriotism and the meaning of wilderness to the Canadian psyche. Climate is implicitly part of such an approach, but rarely is it treated explicitly as having a practical impact on everyday life. W. L. Morton, a strong proponent of the view that Canada was shaped by its "northernness," has observed that Canadian historians ignored winter because they would rather forget about it. Morton himself did little to explain what winter meant in Canadian life other than to observe that the development of a "real outdoor urban life" was limited in Canada because of the climate[2] and that Canadian life was marked by its "northern quality" and a "strong seasonal rhythm."[3] It is apparent, however, that winter's place in the history of leisure in Alberta has been more varied and complex than such general observations suggest. Winter provided unique opportunities for specialized sports, and often created free time for recreation, but at the same time it often brought seasonal unemployment and restricted income, travel and communications. Interwoven with these factors in the years before World War II were technological change and the process of settlement.

It is difficult from our vantage to understand what winter meant to Albertans before World War II. It can be suggested that views of winter have changed, especially in the past twenty years, for we approach winter with a different sense than would have been the case even fifty years ago. The possibility of accessible and relatively cheap winter holidays in hot climes is, if not a reality, then at least a practical hope for many, and the realization of such experiences and the near universal articulation of such ambitions cast winter almost solely in a negative light. Yet for Albertans before World War

II, such an approach to winter would have been remote; most would not have even conceived that an escape from winter was possible, although winter indeed presented major difficulties and discomforts. People often feared prairie winters; the isolation it brought to some was terrifying, and for others its bleakness was demoralizing. One observer in November, 1884, stated that the prairie near Calgary "at this time of the year is dreary, cheerless and sad. I can only compare it to the Libyan desert," and winter was later described with the imagery of death.[4] Despite its drawbacks, however, winter was welcomed by many; the season was rich in social activity and in an agricultural society it brought increased free time, opportunities for leisure activities, and a welcome relief from the labours of summer.

Before 1945 Alberta was largely a rural society. Between 1921 and 1941, about sixty per cent of the population lived on farms or in rural villages,[5] and seasonal change was more significant for such people than it was for those who lived in cities or large towns. Winter provided farmers with greater free time, although this varied greatly depending on the stage of settlement and type of farming practised. In pioneer situations, a house and a barn would have been built immediately on reaching the homestead, but often other buildings would have been erected during winter. Once established, a farm still demanded year-round labour, especially on mixed farms where livestock had to be cared for. Nor was winter wholly free time on grain farms in the southern parts of the province — machinery had to be repaired and draft animals, even if only few in number, maintained. In all cases, securing water and fuel absorbed considerable time and labour. Even so, it is clear that winter provided farmers with more free time and leisure opportunities than did summer. Not all of this free time was given over to leisure pursuits; in many cases, farmers left family behind and worked in bush camps or elsewhere during the winter to make sufficient cash to keep the farm solvent.[6]

For city and town people, the picture was somewhat different. Full-time salaried employees would have had no such seasonal variations in their work and their winter leisure fit around the demands of job and home. For those who took vacations, summer was the time for such activity, and winter holidays were possible only for a privileged few. Costs of travel outside the province or region were high, and the only feasible escape from winter lay in travel to the British Columbia coast. For many urban workers, however, especially those in the construction trades or other seasonal occupations, winter was a time of unemployment, and free time gained at such a cost would hardly be welcomed.[7]

Winter leisure thus varied immensely among different social and economic groups. Yet there were broad patterns of leisure activity that took place in winter, although these activities evolved over time and among different groups in society. Activities strictly dependent on winter were largely confined to sports, although some activities that were not so seasonally specialized, such as dances and community gatherings, often found greatest

expression during winter. In all cases, the unique demands of winter inter-
sected with technological change and the evolution of facilities to shape the
nature of wintertime leisure.

Sport was an obvious focus of winter leisure. The period of greatest
change in winter sport took place during the interwar years when sporting
facilities and organization expanded most significantly. At the turn of the
century, the dominant organized winter sports were curling and, increasingly, hockey. Although preferable, neither required formal facilities. Curling
was initially played on open ice on the river at Edmonton in the late
nineteenth century, and this was likely done in other communities in central and northern Alberta as well.[8] Hockey was also played on open ice, but,
as with curling, the quality of such ice was not ideal and the demarcation
of physical boundaries (other than with snow banks) must have complicated
play. However, private clubs and commercial facilities for both hockey and
curling appeared quickly; both Calgary and Edmonton possessed large and
sophisticated hockey arenas by 1904 and curling rinks had appeared in both
cities by the same time. Until this point, the ice had been dominated by
recreational skaters who were most often unorganized, although there were
a significant number of skating clubs which arranged regular skating parties, dinners and dances as well as fancy-dress skating carnivals.[9] While such
activity continued to be popular, the large commercial rinks forced recreational skaters to take second place to professional and amateur (especially
Senior League) hockey, which was more profitable with its scheduled games
and season tickets for a growing number of spectators.[10] In many communities, public skating rinks were not built until after World War I,
although everywhere local creeks, lakes and sloughs provided an important
focus for unorganized skating.

In the late nineteenth century, hockey was mainly an elite sport organized
through private clubs. The game soon broadened beyond this restricted
focus, and by 1907 its popularity justified the formation of the Alberta
Amateur Hockey Association as the governing body for amateur hockey
in the province. This was the first such association in Western Canada, and
the number of teams expanded rapidly. Hockey suffered a decline during
World War I, but after the war participation increased dramatically and soon
there were few communities without local leagues and teams.[11] In 1940,
Bulmer Watt, the editor of the *Edmonton Journal*, observed that hockey was
increasing in popularity each year and the province was blanketed with
hockey teams.[12]

Like hockey, curling grew rapidly in popularity at the turn of the century,
and by 1904 its play was governed by the Alberta Branch, Royal Caledonian
Curling Club of Scotland. The first curling rink was opened in Edmonton
in 1889, but a great increase in curling facilities occurred just before World
War I. In 1911, the Victoria Curling Club in Calgary, with seventeen sheets
of ice, was the largest curling rink in North America, and by 1922 the five
rinks in Edmonton totalled twenty-nine sheets of ice.[13] By the interwar years,

Hockey rink of the Jesuit College, Edmonton, c. 1926.
Credit: Provincial Archives of Alberta: Photograph Collection A6493.

Hockey rink on the Flats in Edmonton, c. 1914.
Credit: Provincial Archives of Alberta: Brown Collection B6540

smaller facilities were available in most towns, many villages and in some rural communities throughout the province. For many, the annual bonspiel was the highlight of the curling season and the winter social calendar, and bonspiels, like inter-club games, were stimulated by the development of the transportation system in the province during the interwar years. Some curlers travelled far afield to play the game much earlier than this — in 1893 and again in 1903, Edmonton curlers travelled to Winnipeg to compete in bonspiels, and by the turn of the century, inter-club matches between Calgary and Edmonton on Christmas or New Year's Day had become a tradition.[14]

Other sports gained adherents and popularity in the period before World War I. Tobogganing and snowshoeing continued to be popular unorganized winter activities, as they had been from the time of settlement in areas of the province with sufficient snow. However, the most dramatic growth in a snow-based sport was in skiing. Before World War I, skiing had been largely restricted to Scandinavian settlers, but after 1918 its popularity spread beyond these ethnic groups. Although a limited number of skiers had been active at Banff before World War I, a ski resort was not opened there until 1930. At Jasper, development was even slower and only in 1937 did a scheduled "ski train" begin operating to take skiers from Edmonton to Jasper. All these developments signalled the appeal of skiing, although its greatest growth occurred only after World War II.[15]

Indoor sports played in winter also experienced significant growth during the years between the wars. Appropriate facilities were crucial in this case, and court games such as basketball and badminton and activities such as wrestling, boxing, gymnastics and swimming were available in winter only to those with access to indoor facilities. In general terms, this usually meant residents of Calgary, Edmonton, Lethbridge and the largest towns, but rural people too saw court games as having potential for winter leisure. In 1929, Alberta readers of *The Farm and Ranch Review* were told of the great success in one Saskatchewan community of badminton, which, requiring a court 56 by 28 feet, could be accommodated in many community halls.[15] Nevertheless, indoor court games were largely a phenomenon of towns and cities with appropriate facilities, such as those provided by World War I by the Young Men's Christian Association and Young Women's Christian Association in Edmonton, Calgary and Lethbridge. Schools were also sometimes important in this regard; the Raymond Union Jacks, a well-known men's basketball team in the 1920s was a school-based team, as was the even better known Edmonton women's team, the Commercial Graduates Basketball Club.[17]

While opportunities for participation grew, it remains that many farm people had little access to organized winter sports. There was some regional variation in this and it would seem that there was greater mobility and therefore greater possibility for organized winter sports for farm people in southern Alberta than in the central and especially northern parts of the

The McCalla Family skating and tobogganing at Glenbrook Farm, nr. Edmonton, December, 1914. Credit: Provincial Archives of Alberta: Photograph Collection: A9608.

province. In 1928 the provincial government was urged to build all-weather roads in southern Alberta because "the use of the automobile by all classes of communities has become so general."[18] On the other hand, even by the end of World War II it was observed that in central Alberta there was little organized sport in winter for farm people except for those living close to towns[19] — a result of insufficient population for efficient organization, limited transportation and a lack of facilities. Before 1945, organized sports were still a village, town and city luxury and farm people relied upon more individualized or family-oriented games and sports.

Gender distinctions in organized winter sports showed some contrast to summer sports. While women played golf and softball, the other highly popular summer sports — baseball, football, hunting and horse racing — were largely male-dominated. Yet in winter sports, there appears to have been greater overall participation by women. Only hockey was largely a 'male' game, and while there had been a number of women's hockey teams between the wars, by World War II it had become almost exclusively a game for men. The reasons for this change are unclear; it may have been related to the reshaping of hockey into a faster, more aggressive, and therefore, in terms of social stereotypes, more 'male' game or to the reassertion of 'femininity' as a social ideal after World War I.[20] However, other winter sports did not exclude women to the same degree: curling was never seen as especially a 'man's' or a 'woman's' game, recreational skating followed the same pattern, as did skiing and indoor court games.[21] While the exception of hockey was important because of its great popularity, the less rigid exclusion of women in most winter sports merits attention. Perhaps the natural restrictions of winter life made women more insistent on participation, simply because they needed some outdoor physical exercise, or perhaps winter created a more limited pool of players which lessened gender restrictions. It is also possible that winter sports, being less aggressive on the whole (again with the exception of hockey), did not present the same barriers in physical and social terms to women's participation.

Class distinctions are more difficult to understand at this stage of our knowledge of Alberta's sports history. Class and ethnicity were tied closely in Alberta, and social authority was generally linked to ethnicity, with the Anglo-Canadian group having greatest influence and power. All of the popular winter sports, with the exception of skiing, were part of the Anglo-Canadian dominant culture in Alberta. Although the way these sports spread through the society is unclear, it is evident that hockey and curling appealed to a wide range of groups in Alberta, and curling especially, with its Scottish traditions, was seen as part of the assertion of the dominant culture in Alberta.[22] The class and ethnic dimension of indoor court games is less clear. In the case of basketball in southern Alberta, the game was linked to the American origins of many of the settlers, but, in general terms, since court games required relatively expensive facilities, it can be assumed that they were somewhat restricted in ethnic and class terms.

Sport possessed great seasonal specialization, but it was only one aspect of winter leisure. Other popular winter activities were possible year-round, although winter provided an ideal opportunity for their realization. In farm communities especially, winter was a good time for community events because most farmers had more free time. Community dinners, socials and dances were common in most farm communities almost immediately after settlement. In pioneer communities, even in the coldest weather people walked a great deal or got around with horses.[23] The popularity of community events increased further during the interwar years as roads and methods of transportation improved because of the increased use of motor vehicles. While horses continued to be commonly used in many parts of the province up to World War II, cars and trucks — despite the major difficulties their operation in winter presented — helped to widen the scope of community events and the definition of 'community' itself.[24]

These events were a very common form of winter entertainment, especially on weekends in rural communities, but they often depended on having suitable facilities. Schools were often used for such purposes, but they were never entirely adequate because their use was governed by the local school boards and the policies, albeit informal, of the Department of Education.[25] It was only after World War I that community halls began to appear everywhere in the province, a development that greatly encouraged community events.[26] These events, however, varied from community to community. Dancing was an especially popular winter leisure activity in both farm and urban communities, but it was neither universal nor approved of by all people.[27] There was a significant hostility to dancing on religious grounds in some communities, and while many pioneers recall dances as the most popular winter activity, others also recall that they were rare or only developed later. In the community focussed on the Carrit school near Blackfalds, for example, one pioneer recalled that "community dances never occurred until the late years of the first war. Only two or three families danced and they attended such events outside the community." Instead, the community's winter leisure revolved around a "literary society" that met on alternate Friday nights during the winter. "Essentially, the events were social gatherings that ended with a lunch," and their entertainment value was enhanced through songs, recitations, debates, stories and "the reading of a paper called the Rainy Creek Tatler that was actually a list of jokes, jibes, etc. involving individuals present and intended to get a laugh."[28]

While such community events were highly popular, there were additional leisure opportunities even in small towns and especially in the cities. These included movies, fraternal club activities, debates, drama clubs, touring drama troupes and a range of commercial activities such as billiards. Early townspeople saw such events as potentially valuable benefits of town life, and in 1890 it was asked in Lethbridge, "isn't it about time...that a musical or entertainment organization was arranged for here? There is plenty of talent in town for a first-class club or society that will help to make the long winter nights more enjoyable."[29] Such advice was soon unnecessary. Commercial opportunities like pool rooms quickly provided leisure options, although they were not always approved by leaders of opinion. Pool rooms in small towns did most of their business during the winter, and in 1922 it was judged that "the ordinary small village" in Alberta had "no other place of amusement available for its public in the winter" than the pool room.[30] Pool rooms were largely used by adult males although middle-class men would generally have shunned them. For other tastes and groups, drama clubs, musical societies and debating clubs, among others, were also soon operating in many places, and some of these events became winter institutions. For example, mock parliaments, usually held in early winter, were highly popular at the turn of the century, and although their popularity declined and they became less an adult activity and more focussed on older adolescents during the interwar years, they continued to draw wide participation.[31]

Winter carnivals also recognized the place of winter in Canadian life. Although accessible only to a minority of Albertans, such carnivals recognized the need for a community event in celebration of the unique recreational possibilities of winter. Held for the first time in February, 1917, Banff hosted a carnival to promote the winter use of the park and change the popular perception of the townsite as only a summer holiday resort. The carnival ran for ten days and included skating, curling, hockey, swimming races in the Cave and Basin, "pony ski races," trapshooting plus an ice palace presided over by "the snow maidens in their crystal boudoirs."[32] By 1923 the carnival had expanded further to include dog races, a buffalo barbecue and even the movie star dog "Strongheart and his bride-to-be Julie" were in attendance.[33] In a similar fashion, Edmonton held a winter carnival in 1923 that included dances, fancy-dress skating, hockey and other sports, a pageant sponsored by the Hudson's Bay Company of an "attack on Fort Edmonton by Indians," and the coronation of the Queen of the carnival. Most events were held in the arena; 3,000 people attended on a single night, with a further 2,000 turned away for lack of room.[34] Edmontonians seemed to relish the celebration of winter.

In many respects, the calendar of public holidays and days of commemoration reinforced the importance of winter in Alberta's social life. Indeed, winter was sandwiched between public holidays: Thanksgiving in mid-October was the last public holiday before winter, and most Albertans did not accept winter's final end until the May 24 week-end holiday. Between these two signposts lay two of the most significant public holidays for most Albertans, Christmas and Easter, and, along with these, commemorations and celebrations occurred in every winter month. While there were great ethnic variations, for the members of the dominant culture there was Hallowe'en at the end of October, Remembrance Day in November, Robert Burn's Birthday in late January, and, among others, Valentine's Day in February.

Obviously, Christmas was the most important of these holidays and its commercial image, even in the late nineteenth century, idealized its occurrence in winter by emphasizing the beauty of the winter landscape or the contrast of warm homes with snow and cold outside. The significance of Christmas was illustrated by the persistence of ethnic traditions in Christmas food and celebrations. Albertans of Ukrainian descent celebrated Christmas according to the Julian calendar which placed it in mid-January. While this confirmed valuable traditions, it also provided a better mid-way break in a northern winter than did its celebration under the Gregorian calendar. The community side of Christmas was best represented by concerts organized by schools and churches. These festivals were often referred to as "Christmas Trees" in the early twentieth century, and later by the more direct term "Christmas concert" — but all consisted of skits, plays, recitations, music and gifts for the children. Often they concluded with a dance.[35] While Christmas played a central role in social and family life, the other holidays and commemorative days provided significant opportunities for house parties, community celebrations or club festivities. As only one example, Valentine's day was celebrated with parties by at least the mid-1890s in Edmonton, and it continued to be a popular reason for house or club parties.[36]

Christmas, despite its early commercialization, was essentially a home-based celebration, which fit nicely with the importance of the home in winter leisure. Before World War II, there was widespread apprehension among many members of Alberta's dominant culture that modern forms of leisure, such as movies, challenged the authority of the family and the home as the centre of social life. There was, accordingly, great emphasis on home-based leisure to counter these modern tendencies. Despite such idealization, practical consideration such as time, money and transportation inevitably reinforced the home as the centre of winter leisure. Music, cards, and board games were all popular home activities, and reading was seen as pre-eminently a winter pastime, although, as E. A. Corbett of the University of Alberta Department of Extension warned, while "the long winter evenings in Alberta" encouraged reading, it was important that "some guidance should be given as to what is worth reading and what is not."[37] Crafts and hobbies were also popular winter activities for people in all walks of life. The strength of the connection between winter and handicrafts was shown in 1935 when the Alberta Guild of Handicrafts mounted a travelling exhibition of handicrafts both to stimulate and meet public interest in crafts. The display set out by truck in January and included typical items made by Alberta craftspeople: weaving, various needle crafts, pottery, leather work, wood-carving and, among others, hammered copper and brass work.[38] Of all the home-oriented activities, however, the most revolutionary change came through the development of radio during the interwar years.

The first radio station in Alberta was established in 1922 and others were established soon after. The greatest growth in ownership of radios occurred

during the late 1930s and during World War II,[39] but listening to the radio
had become a recognized leisure activity in Alberta by the early 1930s. The
best time for listening to the radio was in the winter when there was less
atmospheric interference and therefore less static, the bane of early radio
reception, and Alberta's cold clear winter nights sometimes permitted
Albertans to enjoy amazing reception of stations throughout North
America.[40] While reception of distant stations was never assured or consistent, Albertans had access to programmes from a number of stations, both
domestic and foreign, to absorb their winter evenings. Many broadcast
schedules were centred around winter: the University of Alberta radio
station CKUA did not operate during the summer, and on North American
commercial stations, the "radio season" (a term in common use by the late
1920s) ran from the fall to the spring, with new shows introduced in September and October. "In the fall," according to one Alberta commentator,
"the young fan's fancy lightly turns to thoughts of — radio, and the touch
of chill in the evening air indicates that the time for long-distance reception
is here."[41] The new line-up for winter was eagerly awaited and reported
widely in newspapers and magazines, often foretelling the pleasures in store
with promises that "the forthcoming season will be the greatest in radio
history."[42] The programming carried on these stations was varied, but
especially popular were American variety and drama programmes. The
establishment of the Canadian Radio Broadcasting Commission in 1932,
followed by the Canadian Broadcasting Corporation in 1936, created a
national broadcasting network that, while carrying some American
programming, also fostered Canadian content.

It might be assumed that radio changed winter leisure patterns by turn-
ing people away from community to home-centred leisure. In 1938 radio was
described by one Albertan as "the chief form of entertainment for the farmer
and family during the winter months."[43] This was doubtless true, but it did
not mean a rejection of community leisure. Rather, radio helped to enrich
weekday evenings when few community events happened in any case. In
1927, the Alberta Wheat Pool began a series of radio broadcasts featuring
news about the Pool, farm issues and farming, as well as performances by
a Glee Club organized among the head-office staff in Calgary. The Pool
asked its listeners what times were best for the broadcast, and a number
forcefully rejected Friday nights "as many people want to go to dances."[44]
Moreover, radio was often integrated into existing community leisure
activities; pie socials and dances were often held to the accompaniment of
the radio,[45] although by the end of World War II such activities would have
become old-fashioned.

Radio, along with changes in transportation, are two examples of the way
that technological change influenced winter leisure, especially during the
interwar years. Radio was a wholly new leisure option, while changes in
transportation influenced participation in more traditional activities. Despite
these changes, it remains that for farm families in some parts of the province

winter brought the vulnerability and loneliness of isolation, and everywhere, houses were often cold and drafty, while seasonal unemployment often meant undernourishment, poverty or the departure of men for winter work in logging camps or mines. Location, occupation and income thus helped to shape Albertans' response to winter.

Yet despite such negative impact, winter also provided change and choice. The season was significant for leisure because it provided many with free time, or at least larger blocks of it, which could be used for leisure opportunities unique to winter, especially in sport. It also provided time and focus for the expression of other activities which, although not unique to winter, found their greatest expression during the long winter. Winter thus directly and indirectly gave leisure a unique expression in Alberta. Community events, various sports and home-centred activities like reading, crafts, listening to the radio, visiting, cards and other games all enlivened winter days and evenings. While the traditions of most settlers gave unique meaning to winter through special activities, festivals, and traditions which occurred during the winter season, the transplantation of these practices was largely a process of adaptation rather than invention in response to the long, cold winters of Alberta.

NOTES

*   The author is a private historian and consultant in historical resources in Edmonton. The sources for this article come from a major study on the history of leisure commissioned by the Historical Resources Division, Alberta Culture and Multiculturalism. A revised version of the study will be published in 1990 as *Useful Pleasures: The Shaping of Leisure in Alberta, 1896-1945*, co-published by Alberta Culture and Multiculturalism and the Canadian Plains Research Centre, University of Regina.

1. Judith Fingard, "The Winter's Tale: The Seasonal Contours of Pre-Industrial Poverty in British North America, 1815-1860," Canadian Historical Association, *Historical Papers, 1974*, 65-94.
2. W. L. Morton, "The 'North' in Canadian Historiography," *Transactions, Royal Society of Canada*, Series IV, vol. 8 (1970/4th Series), 36.
3. W. L. Morton, *The Canadian Identity* (Toronto: University of Toronto Press, 1968), 93.
4. *Edmonton Bulletin*, November 1, 1884; *Farm and Ranch Review*, October 5, 1909.
5. *Alberta Statistical Review Annual. 75th Anniversary Edition* (Edmonton: Alberta Treasury, Bureau of Statistics, 1980), Table 5, p. 6.
6. On supplementary income on mixed farms, see for example, Reynolds Alberta Museum, interviews with C. Schultz and E. Swalling; on the seasonal nature of grain farms see Paul Voisey, *Vulcan: The Making of a Prairie Community* (Toronto: University of Toronto Press, 1988), 158.

7. See for example, *Calgary Herald*, February 22, 1908; *Labour Gazette*, January, 1905, 709; *Census of Canada 1921* vol. III, Table VIII, p. xvii.

8. *Edmonton Bulletin*, November 9, 1889. On open-ice curling at Fort Saskatchewan, see Peter Ream, *The Fort on the Saskatchewan* 2nd edition (n.p.: Metropolitan Printing, 1974), 391-4.

9. See for example, Glenbow Alberta Institute Archives, M16, Allison Collection, diaries and personal papers.

10. See for example, *Calgary Herald*, December 20, 1910.

11. Gary Zeman, *Alberta on Ice* (Edmonton: Westweb Press, 1985), 2, 9, 106, 164, 261.

12. Bruce Peel Special Collection Library, University of Alberta, Watt Collection, Letter, April 20, 1940.

13. Cecil Blackburn, "The Development of Sports in Alberta, 1900-1918" (M.A. thesis, University of Alberta, 1974), 186; *Edmonton Journal*, December 23, 1922. In 1917 northern curlers split away to form the Alberta Curling Association.

14. *Edmonton Bulletin*, January 26, 1893; Nancy and Maxwell Howell, *Sports and Games in Canadian Life* (Toronto: Macmillan, 1969), 172; Blackburn, "The Development of Sports in Alberta, 1900-1918," 177.

15. Rolf Lund, "A History of Skiing in Canada Prior to 1940," (M.A. thesis, University of Alberta, 1971), 163-5, 177-87.

16. *Farm and Ranch Review*, November 15, 1929.

17. Ronald Lappage, "Selected Sports and Canadian Society, 1921-1939" (Ph.D. thesis, University of Alberta, 1974), 51; Carl Betke, "The Social Significance of Sport in the City: Edmonton in the 1920s" in *Cities in the West: Papers of the Western Canadian Urban History Conference* ed A. R. McCormack and I. Macpherson (Ottawa: National Museum of Man, 1975), 225-28.

18. Provincial Archives of Alberta, Premier's Papers, File 295B, City of Lethbridge to Brownlee, July 31, 1928. (Hereafter cited as PAA, PP).

19. Florence Edwards, "Farm Family Living in the Prairie Provinces" (Ottawa: Canada Department of Agriculture, Technical Bulletin 57, 1947), 3.

20. On changes in hockey see Howell and Howell, *Sports and Games*, 213-15.

21. On curling, see P. Voisey, *Vulcan*, 165.

22. On the connection between sport and ethnicity in the prairies, see Morris Mott, "The British Protestant Pioneers and the Establishment of Manly Sports in Manitoba, 1870-1886," *Journal of Sport History* (1980): 27-30.

23. R. G. Moyles (ed), *Challenge of the Homestead. Peace River Letters of Clyde and Myrle Campbell 1919-1924* (Calgary: Alberta Records Publication Board, Historical Society of Alberta, 1988).

24. *The UFA*, July 15, 1929; C. A. Dawson and R. W. Murchie, *The Settlement of the Peace River Country. A Study of a Pioneer Area* (Toronto: The Macmillan Company of Canada Ltd., 1934), 225.

25. See for example, various correspondence in PAA, PP, File 728A, 1936.

26. Orest Martynowych, *The Ukrainian Bloc Settlement in East Central Alberta 1890-1930. A History* (Edmonton: Historic Sites Service, Alberta Culture, Occasional Paper No. 10, 1985), 230-1; PAA 81.177, Namao UFA Community Hall Minute Book, 1925-49 (hereafter cited as PAA).

27. Kathleen Strange, *With the West in Her Eyes* (Toronto: The Macmillan Company of Canada Ltd., 1945), 124.

28. PAA, 76.69, Elsie Gowan Collection, 31-2.

29. *Lethbridge News*, September 24, 1890.

30. PAA, 75.126, Department of the Attorney General, File 732, Browning to Marks, February 3, 1922.

31. See for example, *Edmonton Bulletin*, November 8, 1894; *Camrose Canadian*, December 17, 1908; PAA, PP, File 218, Reid to Greenfield, January 17, 1925.

32. *Calgary Herald*, February 1, 1917.

33. *Red Deer Advocate*, February 9, 1923.
34. *Edmonton Journal*, January 27, 1923.
35. John Blackburn, *Land of Promise* (Toronto: Macmillan, 1970), 194-6.
36. *Edmonton Bulletin*, February 18, 1895; PAA 77.3, Torrance Papers, File 23, "Cupid's Caper," 1945.
37. University of Alberta Archives, 74-23-42, "Some Recent Fiction Worth Reading" n.d. (ca. 1920).
38. University of Alberta, *Report of the Department of Extension for the Year Ending March 31, 1935*, 25-6.
39. PAA, 74.462, Alberta Department of Trade and Commerce, Bureau of Vital Statistics, "Radio Licences;" Bill MacNeil and Morris Wolfe, *The Birth of Radio in Canada — Signing On* (Toronto: Doubleday Ltd., 1982), 155.
40. *Ibid.*, 146.
41. *Farm and Ranch Review*, September 26, 1927.
42. *Ibid.*, September, 1936.
43. *Ibid.*, April, 1938.
44. *The UFA*, August 15, 1927.
45. *Ibid.*, March 11, 1926; *Red Deer Advocate*, April 4, 1924.

WINTER SPORTS IN THE EARLY URBAN ENVIRONMENT OF PRAIRIE CANADA

Carl Betke

At first sight, this is a broad topic with possibilities in many directions, combining five key elements of historical analysis. First, a location, or geography: prairie Canada. Second, a category of community: the city, or at least the urban setting. Third, a time period: "early" in that prairie urban experience. Fourth, a climatic season: winter. And finally, a category of organized activity, an element of culture, a section of the social pattern: sports.

But the effect on defining my topic is more like an intersection than an accumulation: five lines of approach create a pin-point focus of attention. Not just sports, but sports in particular communities in a particular region in winter during a particular period of time. The factor not common in sports history analysis is the reference to season: winter. Major debates in the analysis of sports history have recently tended to connect with four of my five categories, as I shall shortly point out, but not to the importance of season. It may seem, from a consideration of winter together with the prairie region, that the omission should be an obvious fault: prairie winters conjure up a very definite and formidable image, easily distinguished from either prairie summers or Liberian winters. We may recall that the prolific Canadian historian, W. L. Morton, judged the northern climate and environment to be a conditioning factor shaping the Canadian character. We may also recall that his view met with significant criticism.[1] It is this question of the possibility that prairie winters had some unique impact on the urban sporting experience before, say, 1930, that is intriguing.

My approach has been to review the recent literature on the history of modern sport in search of the current perceptions of important issues deserving analysis, to see whether seasonal climate plays any great part in them (it does not); and then to examine the actual experience of sports in Canada's prairie cities during winter time to see what it suggests for the prevailing wisdom. For reasons to be detailed later, the time period under consideration is the half century from 1880 to 1930, right in the middle of the century and a half or so currently commanding the greatest English-language attention to sports history.

High on the study list is the problem of the essence of modern sports as a particular form of recreation, approached from many different angles, all of them tending toward one of two basic but converging positions. One understanding views human social life in dynamic development, with characteristics expected to be markedly different in widely separated periods or traditions. Among the best studies starting from this assumption are books by Peter Bailey and Hugh Cunningham. They offer complex explanations of what both accept as a fundamental transition in late nineteenth-century English sports, tending toward its commercial organization, with a host of ramifications, all seen to be rooted in, and perhaps contributing to, broader socio-economic developments.[2] (Thus, argues Stephen Hardy, if sports in the western world constitutes a modern industry in its own right, let us apply the techniques of business history to understand its recent character.[3]) Looking at the other end of the transition — the result — other scholars like Allen Guttman and Henning Eichberg try to isolate its principal features: among them, role specialization, complex and sustained organization and standardization to maximize artifical tension, an infinity of records quantifying achievements, all promoting long-term interest and thus consumer stability, and widespread distribution of integrated products.[4] Whether or not everyone agrees with the specific portrayal, many agree with the concept that modern sports can be distinguished from preceding recreations.

The other tendency is to lay stress on a primary changelessness rooted in the common psychological requirements of humanity in general. Thus Norbert Elias posits the origins of competitive sports in a basic human need for battle, so fundamental it is not to be extinguished at will, but is to be manifested in forms acceptable to the civilized process by which we accomplish things together.[5] But even here, if the primal urge is suspected to be everywhere and always the same, presumably the civilized forms of its expression vary by society, technical capacity, numbers of people involved, and so on. And there are plenty of avenues to battle in modern history other than sport.

But if sport in recent history has been a manifestation of broader social developments, questions about the average individual's role arise in the same ways as they do for other aspects of social organization. Numerous scholars have investigated the ways communities fracture in their approaches to sports, frequently with obvious distaste for the exclusiveness of practices that have differentiated participation on the basis of income and social status, ethnic identification, or gender.[6] For stratified communities, the possession and exercise of power has received attention, both with respect to efforts at controlling and administering leisure for the greatest perceived good of broader social relationships, and with respect to the mechanisms by which a "hegemony" is established over approved forms of sporting entertainment by influential groups: British Canadians, for example, or a commercial elite.[7] And yet most students of sport history are drawn to the subject by their enjoyment of sporting experiences rather than by a deep-seated repugnance for them. So, for example, both the more positive outlook of historian William Baker and the more critical approach of Canadian sociologist Richard Gruneau perceive the attraction of individual liveliness in recent sport history. They note the tensions between the hope at every social level for a kind of liberating personal experience and the plethora of organizational and commercial devices that have arisen to establish economic and social control.[8]

Among those devices, essentially matters of organization, but in their manifestations exhibiting substantial transformation of the landscape, are the sorts of material features straightforwardly catalogued for the Canadian tradition by Ian Jobling two decades ago: transcontinental transportation systems, urban transportation, a variety of communication media, an industrial workforce in concentrated workplaces, and the institutional results of the premium placed on education and urbanization. These have been expressed in a proliferation of lavish educational structures and facilities for such agencies as elite and fraternal clubs and the Young Men's Christian Association.[9] Together they produced the combination of urban clusters and an urban network, the concentrated purpose of which was to overcome natural obstacles to collective enterprise: both transportation and communication techniques to overcome vast distances; industrial equipment and co-ordinated manpower to extract natural resources and artificially create new forms of material development. With such a framework, one might expect the ultimate urban expression of sports in recent history to feature the co-ordination of large populations and the collective development of forms not possible for small groups, though smaller communities within reach of the urban influence might well feel the impact of urban sports enterprise. Hence various issues of consumerism and spectatorship have emerged in recent historical analyses. Some point to aberrations suggested by the incidence of "hooliganism." Conversely, Morris Mott has, through Winnipeg's example, explored the meaning for spectators of identifying with the best characteristics of young manhood that a particular sponsoring community can produce.[10]

Other works have produced many, and often scathing, revelations of the casualties associated with sport in recent history. They reflect in one way or another the betrayal of rules of organization established to rationalize sports activity. Some of the sinners were no doubt reacting to undemocratic impositions, but some took unfair advantage. In both cases the effect was a continually shifting evolution in the rules of the game, not only for the actual play, but also for the administrative framework.[11] And to suggest yet another area: the historical rationale for the relative exclusion of women has come under increasingly searching examination.[12]

But the purpose of this brief and obviously inadequate review of recent tendencies in the analysis of sport history is to divine the place of the seasons in topics currently winning attention. In fact, nothing in them seems to involve climate. Seasons emerge in recent sport history only in those compilations that catalogue events or developments on a sport-by-sport basis. The recent Howell and Howell volume, which brought together and summarized several of these sorts of studies of Canadian sports, regularly separated winter sports from other categories for each chapter. So also did Wise and Fisher in organizing their material for *Canada's Sporting Heroes.*[13] Keeping in mind the broad thematic analyses we have skimmed over, it is nevertheless possible to derive some further understanding of the relatively modern sports phenomenon through an examination of the prairie urban experience in winter.

We should at the outset understand that the urban criterion fixes the beginning of the relevant period of these reflections in the early 1880s. For an urban context, there must surely be at least sufficient population to remove the mechanisms of community relationships from the style of personal interaction to the style of formal organization, enabling large numbers of relatively anonymous people to function together and deal with the outside world in pursuit of certain common objectives. The selection of 1930 as a closing date is in part an arbitrary decision to impose analytical control, although the 1930s serve as a convenient watershed in the purely demographic and physical growth pattern of prairie cities. Were we to set a population of 10,000 as minimum, Winnipeg qualified by the mid-1880s, but Calgary, Edmonton and Brandon did not until after 1905, and Regina, Moose Jaw, Saskatoon and briefly Lethbridge not until sometime around 1910. But in order to be able to consider 1920s populations of an even higher order (more than 30,000), Winnipeg, Edmonton, Calgary, Regina and Saskatoon constitute the sample: Winnipeg with its suburbs approaching a population of 225,000 by 1926; Edmonton and Calgary each more than 65,000; Regina and Saskatoon each between 30,000 and 40,000.[14] On the evidence of both age and size, Winnipeg clearly was consistently a city of superior scale and complexity within the region.

We now come up against the very tricky question of what constitutes a winter sport, and it is illuminating just to notice such a dilemma. We could limit the list to those activities that were possible only during the winter, or we could accept all those that were commonly enjoyed during the winter months, omitting those for which the outdoor environment of the region's summer was required. In fact, there is excellent reason in the context of this discussion to follow the latter course, because so much of the prairie urban winter sports experience came in the form of indoor games like basketball and badminton.

The first obvious condition of sports in the early prairie cities was its diversity. In addition to whatever matches were organized on the spur of the moment or by neighbours without formal trappings, the organized opportunities proliferated in hockey, curling, ski jumping, boxing, basketball, bowling, pool and billiards, skating, snowshoeing, volleyball, badminton, table tennis, swimming, roller skating, wrestling, and some others less regularly. Such activities as were available at smaller centres were probably not as readily available; that is, hockey would not be offered at so many levels and be supported by so many sponsors. In the cities, hockey opportunities abounded in church, mercantile (with commercial or industrial sponsors), school, YMCA, university, women's, senior men's, intermediate men's, juvenile boys' and midget boys' leagues. By the early 1930s, about 120 teams of boys under 20 played provincially organized hockey in Winnipeg.[16]

Should we turn back to one of the two popular winter sports of Winnipeg at Christmas time, 1886, in a city of some 20,000, we would notice the ascendancies of an entirely different sport, but the beginnings of the same tradition of organization. Snowshoeing was organized by three distinct clubs: the St. George's Club, oldest (since 1879) and largest; the Winnipeg Snowshoe Club, not half the size of the pioneer club but planning to add a toboggan slide; and the fledgling St. Boniface Club. All told, membership ran close to 1,000, a figure leading to the local claim that, next to Montreal, Winnipeg was "the greatest centre for winter sports in Canada." On three separate evenings a week the respective memberships went out on their regular "tramps," and between times they organized gala festivities like receptions for the other clubs.[17]

A fierce commitment to curling provided the remaining weight of Winnipeg's claim to winter sporting supremacy. Curling is a particularly apt game through which to examine the difference between urban and rural winter sports: it was popular in both kinds of communities, but the city provided a bewildering selection of opportunities. Many commentators have

Outing of the St. George's Snowshoe Club, Winnipeg, 1885.
Credit: Provincial Archives of Manitoba, Events 4 Collection, N5957

reported the multi-faceted arrangements presented in the curling organization of early prairie cities. Club membership over-arched rink membership
in providing the context for regular club competition; but beyond that,
bonspiels provided inter-club competition among rinks according to a
concentrated tournament format, and many of the bonspiels featured inter-
community play bringing rinks from outside centres. The number of
interlocking events and the large number of prizes provided an ongoing sense
of involvement and variety. From 1889 the annual Winnipeg bonspiel was
the undisputed jewel of the entire system for western Canada and one of the
two most distinguished events in Canada. With the best facilities, both inside
and outside the rink and for spectators as well as participants, the city clubs
dominated as bonspiel hosts for major events like provincial championships.
If the champions did not always come from the city, they always curled
there: their sport was drawn in to the city.[18]

Similar cases can certainly be made for the winter sports that gained
popularity a little later: basketball, for example, and badminton. The
Mormon concentration on basketball in southern Alberta provided the
exception setting out the rule in relief: that each city contained the population and had the facilities (especially those provided early by the YMCA and
increasingly by the schools) to make whole leagues of teams viable within
their own boundaries, contributing the collective experience from which to
select representative teams to play in a wider arena. It is not so much the fact
that a Winnipeg team won the 1927 national men's championship that proves
my point; it is the participation of 29 teams in the Calgary public school girls'
league.[19] With respect to badminton, we know from reports on Winnipeg
and Calgary that interest and participation in badminton emerged during
the 1920s, in clubs and ordinary schools, churches and community hall
facilities alike. The strength of support permitted the Calgary Badminton
Club to erect a special new building in time to host the 1931 provincial
badminton championships.[20]

With greater population bases, the prairie cities possessed greater capacities for achieving artificiality than did rural communities; for escaping
nature with ameliorating facilities. It is the essence of civic pride to point to
impressive improvements on original conditions, and the development of
urban sports was accompanied by the construction of edifices that increasingly helped to distinguish prairie cities from nearby villages and towns.
Calgary skaters and hockey players had played in quite a variety of covered
rinks from the 1880s, but none compared with the Calgary Auditorium Rink,
later known as the Sherman Rink, built in 1904 and adaptable, among other
options, to roller skating and roller hockey. Ten years later athletic club
facilities were added: proper dressing rooms and showers, a larger ice sur-
face and the critical innovation of artificial ice. (A year earlier, in 1913, two
professional exhibition hockey games between teams from Vancouver and
New Westminster, and then Quebec and an eastern all-star team, had
deteriorated in the slush of late March and early April.) A fire demolished

Hockey Team in Sherman Rink, Calgary, 1908 or 1909.
Credit: Glenbow-Alberta Institute Archives, NA2354-13

the Sherman Rink in February, 1915, but a few years later another of the Calgary rinks (Crystal) was similarly upgraded.[21]

In 1914, Regina's Victoria Hockey Club won the Allan Cup for the Canadian Senior Men's championship. The publicity material boasted of Regina's "World Amateur Champions," but also showed off "the Amphitheatre, Regina's Municipal Rink and Fair Building, and undoubtedly the finest hockey arena in the world," with an ice sheet 85' by 220', and a seating capacity of 5,600, built at a total cost of $130,000.[22] The Edmonton Gardens, originally built by the Exhibition Association as its Livestock Pavilion, but designed in close consultation with Edmonton's chief hockey promoters, boasted a similar magnificence.[23] These, and major curling rinks, impressive schools with gymnasium features, a large YMCA facility in each city — all were urban contributions to prairie winter sport.

The concentration of sporting populations and the facilities they supported made prairie cities the settings for the commercial promotion of sports, recreation and entertainment even before World War I. Commercial bowling alleys proliferated, as the burgeoning urban populations suggested the possibilities for establishments similar to what Tommy Ryan had developed in Toronto: a recreational service that could, through recreational leagues of teams of bowlers, be promoted to an increasing flock of patrons. Ryan's five-pin innovation, developed specifically to meet the needs expressed by consumers, caught on quickly, so that by the 1920s thousands of bowlers were regularly active in prairie cities every winter.[24] To a certain extent, the same was true for pool and billiards establishments, initially in connection with hotels, and then in separate halls, but the image of pool halls could not be disassociated from gambling, drinking and male dissolution. The tours of travelling English champions threatened to enhance the respectability of billiards just before the war, but the era of prohibition simply emphasized the liquor connection and maintained the division between the tradition of billiards at the gentlemen's clubs and the impression of dissipation attached to the commercial establishments.[25]

The increase in organized sports activities contributed to another commercial adjunct, the manufacturing and distribution of equipment and supplies. Calgary's billiards supplies, like most other imports, came from Winnipeg, and it would make an interesting study to examine the nature of the sporting goods business in prairie Canada, to notice distinctions that might apply to winter sports materials.

The best known business opportunities were the most public ones: the promotion of sporting spectacles for audiences that would pay to make them profitable or at least viable. Countless examples emerged in many different areas. When Tommy Burns, former world heavyweight boxing champion, came to Calgary in 1910 (subsequently to set up residence there with a haberdashery), it was to provide a running commentary on a novel moving-picture show of the recent Jack Johnson — Jim Jeffries world heavyweight championship boxing match. But he stayed for a few years to train for

Paddy White's Pool Parlors and Bowling Alleys, Saskatoon, 1910.
Credit: Saskatoon Public Library — Local History Room.

Tommy Burns, Calgary Boxer and Fight Promoter, previously World Heavyweight Boxing Champion.
Credit: Glenbow-Alberta Institute Archives, NA1451-40

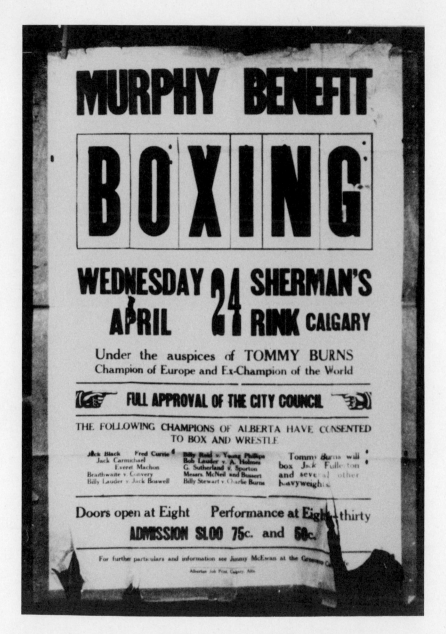

Poster for Boxing Match arranged by Tommy Burns, Calgary.
Credit: Glenbow-Alberta Institute Archives, NA3496-12

occasional fights of his own and stage others between imported fighters, garnering private financial support to erect his own Manchester Arena. His sojourn was typical of the pattern for many other prize fighters who moved from place to place, but settled down for a year or two or three to use one of the prairie cities as a temporary place of training and identification. Burns, born Noah Brusso in Hanover, Ontario, simply had the advantage in publicity of his three-year period of fame and the notoriety of his agreement to be the first champion to defend his title against, and lose, to a black boxer.[27]

I have in other articles raised the name of "Deacon" White, the industrious promoter of team sports spectacles in Edmonton before and after World War I.[28] Though he arrived as a minor league baseball player and naturally worked into the managerial and promotional end of professional baseball, he turned his attention to any sport that showed promise, whether he knew anything about it or not: thus, his name is associated with Edmonton hockey teams as well as with baseball and football. There is no better example of his vision than his promotion of the first Edmonton Grads challenge match against the acknowledged women's champion team from Cleveland in 1923 at the Edmonton Arena. For eight years the Grads' status as Alberta, and later Canadian, champions had gone unheralded; but this new approach launched them into the limelight, particularly in Edmonton itself where they were lionized for the identification with excellence they brought to the Edmonton reputation.[28] But notice how similar the technique of promotion was in some ways (by no means all!) to the promotion of prize fights: in both cases the champion took on the challenge of ambitious rivals, and the image of world championship created the focus of attention.

Two asides may provoke interesting new lines of investigation. The women's hockey teams of the prairie cities may also have been the best in the world,[30] but presumably the absence of challengers from outside the country diminished the prospects for promoting that talent. And on the Grads themselves: they stand out as very unusual champions to attain such adulation, since they were women. This bothered none other than the inventor of basketball himself, Dr. James Naismith. The Grads avoided the straight jacket of "girls rules" basketball: they played "boys rules." In a 1925 letter to Grads coach Percy Page, Naismith revealed his anxiety lest "the boys' style of game affected the social attributes and general health of your players," but on meeting them, he reported, he was greatly pleased to find "these young ladies exhibiting as much grace and poise at an afternoon tea as vigorous ability on the basketball court." He credited Mrs. Page with that, but congratulated all on "such marked success...while retaining their fine womanly instincts."[31]

Finally, the promotion of inter-city sport created the possibility and impetus for importing excellent players, a feat accomplished most readily by offering some sort of inducement, ultimately a financial one. Controversies raged repeatedly before World War I in several prairie cities over the travesty of representative senior hockey teams operating with so-called "travelling" players whose shifting loyalties, it seemed obvious, could only be explained by monetary inducements. The settling-out period, after the introduction of the Allan Cup in 1908 to distinguish the amateur championship from Stanley Cup professional play, produced regular antagonism before World War I and a much clearer distinction afterward. The result on the prairies was the acceptance of professional hockey from 1920 to 1927 in most if not all centres. With it came such established professional hockey stars of central Canada as Edouard "Newsy" Lalonde at Saskatoon.[32]

That the small prairie cities could support professional hockey for even that length of time is probably a result of the brief delay before the possibilities of Canada's winter game were fully grasped in large American centres. Here we get at a major winter sports contribution of western Canadian cities: the development, complete packaging, and demonstration of the professional product, easily lured out of the west by superior markets and therefore superior resources elsewhere. By the complete packaging I mean, above all else, the packaging of winter itself. What was the chief drawback to the commercial organization of hockey before World War I? Slushy ice! Natural conditions would not allow a predictable playing season, particularly at playoff time, and particularly in Calgary with its uncertain winter. So where was the innovation of artificial ice pioneered? Where the demand existed but the natural conditions prevented play: in Vancouver, closely followed by Toronto and Victoria. Then prairie cities caught on to the last stage in artificiality demanded by their game. Once demonstrated, it was swept away, Duke Keats, Bill and Bun Cook, and all.[33]

In the end, the particularly *urban* aspect of winter sports on the prairies boiled down to three essentials: first, the structures and associated facilities that either defeated or reproduced winter in a sheltered, controlled environment permitting complex rational organization of winter sports events; second, the great number and variety of organized sports events, accessible both to participants and spectators from within and outside the city; and third, the concentration of prospects, consumers and facilities that frequently raised the possibility of expert or even professsional teams representing the city against representative teams from other similar centres. The development of facilities and the careers of commercial sports promoters deserve more concentrated study as a unique aspect of prairie urban development. We know little about them except that prairie winters did indeed mean something to their enterprises.

Saskatoon Sheiks Professional Hockey Team, ca. 1924-1926. Player-Manager, Edouard "Newsy" Lalonde, from the Montreal Canadiens, fourth from left. Credit: Saskatoon Public Library — Local History Room.

NOTES

1. W. L. Morton, "'The North' in Canadian Historiography," *Transactions, Royal Society of Canada,* Fourth Series, vol. 8 (1970), 31-40. I recall the professor's doubt in a graduate class that northern-ness had much impact on the vast majority of Canada's residents.
2. Peter Bailey, *Leisure and Class in Victorian England: Rational Recreation and the Contest for Control, 1830-1885* (Toronto: University of Toronto Press/London: Routledge and Kegan Paul, 1978); Hugh Cunningham, *Leisure in the Industrial Revolution c.1780-c.1880* (London: Croom Helm, 1980).
3. Stephen Hardy, "Entrepreneurs, Organization and the Sport Marketplace: Subjects in Search of Historians," *Journal of Sport History,* vol. 13, no. 1 (Spring, 1986), 15-31.
4. Allen Guttmann, *From Ritual to Record: The Nature of Modern Sports* (New York: Columbia University Press, 1978), and Guttmann's discussion of Henning Eichberg's works in German in "Recent Work in European Sport History," *Journal of Sport History,* vol. 10, no. 1 (Spring, 1983), 47-48.
5. Norbert Elias, "Introduction," in Norbert Elias and Eric Dunning, *Quest for Excitement* (Oxford/New York: Basil Blackwell, 1986), 19-62.
6. Alan Metcalfe, *Canada Learns to Play: The Emergence of Organized Sport 1807-1914* (Toronto: McClelland and Stewart, 1987); Eileen Yeo and Stephen Yeo, eds., *Popular Culture and Class Conflict 1590-1914: Explorations in the History of Labour and Leisure* (Sussex: The Harvester Press, 1981); Roy Rosenzweig, *Eight Hours for What We Will: Workers and Leisure in an Industrial City, 1870-1920* (Cambridge: Cambridge University Press, 1983); Stephen Hardy, "The City and the Rise of American Sport: 1820-1920," *Exercise and Sports Sciences Reviews,* vol. 9 (1981), 183-219; J. A. Mangan and Roberta J. Park, eds., *From "Fair Sex" to Feminism: Sport and the Socialization of Women in the Industrial and Post-Industrial Eras* London, England/Totowa, N. J.: Frank Cass, 1987); David K. Wiggins, "Clio and the Black Athlete in America: Myths, Heroes and Realities," *Quest,* vol. 32 (1980), 217-225.
7. Peter C. McIntosh, "An Historical View of Sport and Social Control," *International Review of Sport Sociology,* vol. 6 (1971), 5-13; S. J. Parry, "Hegemony and Sport," *Journal of the Philosophy of Sport,* vol. 10 (1984), 71-83; Alan Ingham and Stephen Hardy, "Sport: Structuration, Subjugation, and Hegemony," *Theory, Culture and Society,* vol. 2 (1984), 85-104; John Hargreaves, *Theatre of the Great: Sport and Hegemony in Britain* (Oxford: Blackwell, 1985); Hart Cantelon and Richard Gruneau, eds., *Sport, Culture and the Modern State* (Toronto: University of Toronto Press, 1982); Metcalfe, *Canada Learns;* and see references in William J. Baker, "The State of British Sport History," *Journal of Sport History,* vol. 10, no. 1 (Spring, 1983), 58-60. For a western Canadian application, see D. G. Wetherell and I. R. A. Kmet, *Useful Pleasures: The Shaping of Leisure in Alberta 1896-1945* (Regina: Alberta Culture and Multiculturalism/Canadian Plains Research Center, forthcoming 1990).
8. William J. Baker, *Sports in the Western World* (Totowa, N. J.: Rowman and Littlefield, 1982), 334-339; Richard Gruneau, "Freedom and Constraint: The Paradoxes of Play, Games and Sports," *Journal of Sport History,* vol. 7, no. 3 (Winter, 1980), 68-86; Richard Gruneau, *Class, Sports and Social Development* (Amherst: University of Massachusetts Press, 1983), 50-51, 142-153.
9. Ian F. Jobling, "Urbanization and Sport in Canada, 1867-1900," in Richard S. Gruneau and John G. Albinson, eds., *Canadian Sport: Sociological Perspectives* (Don Mills: Addison-Wesley (Canada) Limited, 1976), 64-77.
10. Morris Mott, "Flawed Games, Splendid Ceremonies: The Hockey Matches of the Winnipeg Vics, 1890-1903," *Prairie Forum,* vol. 10, no. 1 (1985), 182-184; Morris Mott, "The British Protestant Pioneers and the Establishment of Manly Sports in Manitoba, 1870-1886," *Journal of Sport History,* vol. 7, no. 3 (Winter, 1980), 25-36; Allen Guttmann, *Sports Spectators* (New York: Columbia University Press, 1986); Donald G. Kyle, Melvin

L. Adelman and Allen Guttmann, "Spectators and Crowds in Sports History: A Critical Analysis of Allen Guttmann's *Sports Spectators,*" *Journal of Sport History,* vol. 14, no. 2 (1987), 209-225; Joe Maguire, "Images of Manliness and Competing Ways of Living in Late Victorian and Edwardian Britain," *British Journal of Sports History,* vol. 3, no. 3 (December, 1986), 265-287; Peter Levine and Peter Vinten-Johansen, "Sports Violence and Social Crisis," in Donald Spivey, ed., *Sport in America: New Historical Perspectives* (Westport, Conn.: Greenwood Press, 1985); and see references in Baker, "The State," 60.

11. Stephen A. Riess, *Touching Base: Professional Baseball and American Culture in the Progressive Era* (Westport, Conn.: Greenwood Press, 1980); Eliot Asinoff, *Eight Men Out: The Black Sox and the 1919 World Series* (New York: Holt, Rinehart and Winston, 1963); David Quentin Voigt, *American Baseball: From the Commissioner to Continental Expansion* (Norman: University of Oklahoma Press, 1970); Mott, "Flawed Games."

12. Roberta J. Park, "Sport, Gender and Society in a Transatlantic Victorian Perspective," in Mangan and Park, eds., *From "Fair Sex,"* 58-93; Stephanie L. Twin, ed., *Out of the Bleachers: Writings on Women and Sport* (Old Westbury, N. Y.: The Feminist Press, 1979); Laura Robincheaux, "An Analysis of Attitudes Towards Women Athletes in the U. S. in the Early Twentieth Century," *Canadian Journal of History of Sport and Physical Education,* vol. 6 (May, 1975), 12-22; William H. Beazley and Joseph P. Hobbs, "'Nice Girls Don't Sweat': Women in American Sport," *Journal of Popular Culture,* vol. 16, no. 4 (1982), 42-53.

13. Maxwell L. Howell and Reet Howell, eds., *History of Sport in Canada* (Champaign, Ill.: Stipes Publishing Co., 1981); S. F. Wise and Douglas Fisher, *Canada's Sporting Heroes* (Don Mills: General Publishing Co., 1974).

14. A. F. J. Artibise, ed., *Town and City: Aspects of Western Canadian Urban Development* (Regina: Canadian Plains Research Center, 1981), 430.

15. Metcalfe, *Canada Learns,* 99-132; Carl Betke, "The Social Significance of Sport in the City: Edmonton in the 1920s," in A. R. McCormack and Ian Macpherson, eds., *Cities in the West* (Ottawa: National Museums of Canada, 1975), 213-220; Carl Betke, "The Original City of Edmonton: A Derivative Prairie Urban Community," in Artibise, ed., *Town and City,* 339-342; J. William Brennan, ed., *Regina Before Yesterday: A Visual History 1882 to 1945* (Regina: City of Regina, 1978), 191.

16. Ronald Lappage, "The Canadian Scene and Sport, 1921-1939," in Howell and Howell, eds., *History of Sport,* 251.

17. Wise and Fisher, *Canada's Sporting Heroes,* 16-18; Kevin Jones, "Sports and Games from 1900-1920," in Howell and Howell, eds., *History of Sport,* 207; Edith Paterson, comp., *Winnipeg 100* (Winnipeg: Winnipeg Free Press, 1973), 15; *Manitoba Daily Free Press,* November 3, 5, 11, 1886.

18. *Manitoba Daily Free Press,* November 6, 1886; *Winnipeg Daily Tribune,* February 1, 1890; Gerald Redmond, *The Sporting Scots of Nineteenth-Century Canada* (London/Toronto: Associated University Presses, 1982), 104-158; A. F. J. Artibise, *Winnipeg: An Illustrated History* (Toronto: James Lorimer and Company/National Museum of Man, 1977), 88,90,98; Paterson, comp., *Winnipeg 100,* 15; Betke, "The Social Significance," 217; Brennan, ed., *Regina,* 55, 129; W. A. Riddell, *Regina From Pile O' Bones to Queen City of the Plains: An Illustrated History* (Burlington, Ontario: Windsor Publications (Canada) Ltd., 1981), 65-66, 153; W. M. McLennan, *Sport in Early Calgary* (Calgary: Fort Brisebois Publ., 1983), 245-275; Wetherell and Kmet, *Useful Pleasures.*

19. E. B. Mitchelson, "The Evolution of Men's Basketball in Canada 1892-1936" (Unpublished M.A. Thesis, University of Alberta, 1968), 56; McLennan, *Sport,* 83-92; Jones, "Sports and Games," 194-195; Lappage, "The Canadian Scene," 225.

20. Lappage, "The Canadian Scene," 254-255; McLennan, *Sport,* 371.

21. McLennan, *Sport,* 102-127; Tom Moore et. al., "History of Sport in Calgary," in Elsie C. Morison and P. N. R. Morison, eds., *Calgary 1875-1950* (Calgary: Calgary Publ. Co., 1950), 146; Tom Ward, *Cowtown: An Album of Early Calgary* (Calgary: City of Calgary Electric System/McClelland and Stewart West, 1975), 418; Wetherell and Kmet, *Useful Pleasures.*

22. Brenda Zeman, *Hockey Heritage: 88 Years of Puck-Chasing in Saskatchewan* (Regina: WDS Association/Saskatchewan Sports Hall of Fame, 1983), 36-39; Riddell, *Regina From Pile O' Bones*, 108.
23. Carl Betke, "Sports Promotion in the Western Canadian City: The Example of Early Edmonton," *Urban History Review*, vol. 12, no. 2 (October, 1983), 53.
24. Wise and Fisher, *Canada's Sporting Heroes*, 273-274; Betke, "The Social Significance," 214-215; Jones, "Sports and Games," 195-196; Lappage, "The Canadian Scene," 253-254; McLennan, *Sport*, 284-294; Moore, "History of Sport," 147.
25. *Manitoba Free Press Weekly*, December 16, 1886; McLennan, *Sport*, 367-370; Betke, "Sports Promotion," 50; Artibise, *Winnipeg*, 62; Brennan, ed., *Regina*, 139; Wetherell and Kmet, *Useful Pleasures*.
26. McLennan, *Sport*, 367-370.
27. For background on Burns, see Richard Broome, "The Australian Reaction to Jack Johnson, Black Pugilist," in Richard Cashman and Michael Mckernan, eds., *Sport in History* (St. Lucia: University of Queensland Press, 1979), 343-363; Wise and Fisher, *Canada's Sporting Heroes*, 137-139; Jones, "Sports and Games," 197. For Burns in Calgary, see McLennan, *Sport*, 190-215; Moore, "History of Sport," 149; Max Foran and Heather MacEwan Foran, *Calgary: Canada's Frontier Metropolis: An Illustrated History* (Calgary: Windsor Publications Inc., 1982), 130, 188.
28. Betke, "Sports Promotion," 48,53-54.
29. Betke, "The Social Significance," 223-225.
30. Zeman, *Hockey Heritage*, 251-264; Margaret Ann Hall, "A History of Women's Sport in Canada Prior to World War I" (Unpublished M.A. Thesis, University of Alberta, 1968), 176; McLennan, *Sport*, 102-127; Wetherell and Kmet, *Useful Pleasures*.
31. Dr. James Naismith to J. Percy Page, July 8, 1925: Edmonton Grads Papers, Provincial Archives of Alberta, 70.27.
32. Don Kerr and Stan Hanson, *Saskatoon: The First Half-Century* (Edmonton: NeWest Press, 1982), 256-258; Metcalfe, *Canada Learns*, 168-172; Wise and Fisher, *Canada's Sporting Heroes*, 70-71.
33. Metcalfe, *Canada Learns*, 171; McLennan, *Sport*, 102-127; Jones, "Sports and Games," 199, 202; Lappage, "The Canadian Scene," 249-250; Moore, "History of Sport," 146, 149; Riddell, *Regina From Pile O' Bones*, 65-66.

THE EDMONTON COMMERCIAL GRADUATES: WOMEN'S HISTORY: AN INTEGRATIONIST APPROACH

Elaine Chalus

Every coach dreams of coaching an award-winning record-setting team — every athlete dreams of playing on such a team. In the past few years, Edmonton has been fortunate enough to have both the coaches and the athletes necessary to create this winning combination. The glories achieved by the Oilers and the Eskimos, however, are not Edmonton's only claim to fame. Between 1915 and 1940, Edmonton was the home of one of the most enduring sports dynasties ever created: the Edmonton Commercial Graduates. The statistics speak for themselves. The Grads were the provincial champions for twenty-three out of twenty-four years, the Western Canadian Champions from 1926 to 1940, and the Canadian champions from their first title attempt in 1922 until they disbanded in 1940. They won the Underwood International Trophy for Canada-United States competition consecutively from its introduction in 1923 until 1940, and they swept all twenty-seven international exhibition games played in conjunction with four sets of Olympic Games. In a twenty-five year period, the Grads won 96.2% of the 522 games they played.[1] Statistical excellence is one thing; however, the fact that the Grads were not only from Edmonton, but an Edmonton women's basketball team, makes them truly outstanding in both athletic and women's history.

As an exceptional athletic team, the Grads earned a legitimate place in the annals of sports' history; as a Canadian women's phenomenon, they merit the attention of women's historians. Traditional historical analysis tends to emphasize the political and economic power structures of a society, and since women's position in Western society has traditionally excluded them from active participation in these power structures, history has become a male-oriented and male-dominated discipline. In order to redress this imbalance, women must be reintegrated into history. Neither women nor men exist in gender isolation, and as such, a balanced historical view should attempt to integrate the male and female historical experiences in order to form a coherent and balanced whole. This goal cannot be attained unless both the historical experience of women and their achievements are retrieved and preserved. In an effort to begin this process of reintegration, this paper will be divided into two parts: the first part will present the Grads as an historical fact; the second part will attempt to explore the differences between feminist and integrationist historical approaches to the Grads' experience.

I

Every legend has its origin in actual experience, and the Grads are no exception. It is very probable that the Edmonton Grads would never have been formed had J. Percy Page not lost a coin toss with Ernest E. Hyde in 1914. Both young men were teachers at McDougall Commercial High School, and since neither felt prepared to teach physical education to sixty girls, the coin toss decided the issue. Although Page was not an accomplished basketball player, he was methodical and quickly developed a systematic teaching approach. This concentration on fundamentals paid off, as his team ended its first season as the undefeated city champions. In 1915, Page's girls went on to win the provincial championships against the Camrose Normal School. The Edmonton Commercial Graduates Basketball Team evolved as a result of Page's success in interesting girls in the game of basketball. In the spring of 1915, a group of the graduating members of the provincial championship team approached Page about forming a graduates' team, in order that they might continue to play basketball after graduating from school. Page acquiesced, and on June 15, 1915, the Grads were formed.[2]

Unlike other award-winning teams which switch coaches and recruit players in hopes of improving their chances, the Grads' existence was characterized by a sense of permanence and immutability. All but two of the girls who played as Grads were actually graduates of McDougall Commmercial, and all of the Grads' teams were coached by Dr. Page. Throughout the team's twenty-five year existence, McDougall Commercial's tiny gymnasium continued as the main practice venue, although Varsity gymnasium was used prior to international games to allow the team to practice on a regulation size court. Once the team became popular, these practices were nearly as much of a spectator attraction as the games, which were held in front of immense crowds at the Edmonton Arena. In order to ensure sufficient talent for future Grads' teams, Page developed a feeder system within McDougall Commercial. Girls who were interested in basketball began playing on junior teams, and then progressed to senior teams. If they were talented, they could then be chosen to become members of the official feeder team, the Gradettes. The transition from the Gradettes to the Grads was not inevitable, as talent by itself was not enough to merit a spot on the team: in order for a girl to be chosen, she had to fit Page's conception of a woman athlete. The Grads were expected to be "ladies first, athletes second,"[3] and while this meant that some extremely talented players never became Grads, it also ensured that the personality profile and makeup of the Grads' teams remained remarkably consistent.[4] The other factor that limited the number of girls who could become Grads was the fact that outgoing team members were replaced, by position, only as they retired or married.[5] As a result, in twenty-five years there were only thirty-eight Grads.[6]

The Grads were also different from other contemporary women's basketball teams, especially those in the United States, because they were an entirely amateur team. At no point in the Grads' existence did they accept corporate sponsorship, and none of the players ever received financial assistance. The Grads were all working girls — mainly stenographers, bookkeepers, and sales clerks — who were forced to take their vacations or take time off without pay in order to participate on trips. Funding for travel came directly from box-office receipts. The team's amateur status was carefully guarded by Page, who perceived it to be as important as his fundamental tenets of good sportsmanship and ladylike behaviour.[7]

From 1915 to 1922, the Grads were an entirely local concern. In order to find enough competition, they played both men and women's teams, switching from the less demanding girls' rules to the more generally accepted boys' rules just prior to undertaking their first major challenge in 1922. With classic, central-Canadian tunnel vision, the London Ontario Shamrocks had claimed the 1922 Dominion Championship without even considering the possibility of western competition. The Grads protested, and in a move that would have warmed the cockles of W. L. Morton's heart, they scrounged up barely enough money to take six players (no substitutes) with boxed lunches to Ontario by day coach. In four days, they won all four games they played, and returned to Edmonton as the new Dominion Basketball Champions. This win marked the beginning of the Grads' popularity. Although their first home-exhibition game after the championship win netted only $20.00 profit, they did gain popularity. The team was met at the train station by a crowd of fans and a band, and were later presented with gold medals at a school board fete given in their honour. Edmonton's attention had been captured by their singular achievement.[8]

The Grads' 1922 accomplishment encouraged a local promoter to organize the first international women's basketball series for the Underwood Challenge Trophy in 1923. If the 1922 Dominion Championship had been the team's initiation, this series against the "World Champs," Cleveland Favourite-Knits, was the team's graduation. In spite of the fact that the Edmonton girls looked decidedly old-fashioned in their middies and pleated bloomers, they were quite capable of holding their own against the more fashionably-garbed competition. Two decisive victories gave the Grads the international trophy, and started a tradition. By the time the trophy was permanently awarded to the Grads in 1940, they had won 114 of the 120 Underwood games, and had never allowed the trophy to slip from their possession.[9]

The Underwood series translated into Grad popularity. It also increased their ambition. Edmonton was a small city in the 1920s, and the Grads were a local phenomenon. The team was presented with medals and gifts, and

Commercial Grads Basketball team, Edmonton, 1923. First winners of the
Underwood International Trophy.
Credit: Provincial Archives of Alberta: Photograph Collection A11413.

Page was given a brand new Chevrolet coupe by local businessmen who felt
that the Grads' success had been excellent publicity for Edmonton and a
definite boost to Edmonton businesses.[10] Many other coaches and teams
would have been content with this sort of recognition and their provincial,
Dominion, and international titles, but the Grads were an unusual team.
Page lobbied to have women's basketball accepted as an official Olympic
sport for the 1924 Paris Olympics, but was not successful. The Grads were,
however, invited to take part in the Olympic exhibition games. The price
tag for the trip to Europe was $11,000.00. There are many modern coaches
who would blanch at the thought of attempting to raise this sum, abandon-
ing the idea of international competition as interesting but impossible: —
Page did not. By the time of the Olympics, the team had raised sufficient
funds to take all eight players and their coach, as well as Mrs. Page who
acted as chaperone. The Grads' trip to the Paris Olympics was the beginning of another winning streak. By the time the team disbanded in 1940, they
had attended four Olympic Games (Paris, 1924; Amsterdam, 1928; Los
Angeles, 1932; and Berlin, 1936). They also won all twenty-seven of the
international exhibition games that they played.[11]

Edmonton Commercial Grads Basketball team, en route to Paris, 1924.
Credit: Provincial Archives of Alberta: Photograph Collection A11414.

Between 1925 and 1940, the Grads reigned supreme. They hosted eastern and American teams, and travelled across Canada and the United States in search of competition. To perfect their skills prior to trips and matches, they practiced against the Gradettes one night a week and the Boy Grads another night.[12] On nine separate occasions, they were pitted against men's teams; they won seven of these games for a 78% average.[13] With a 147-game winning streak followed directly by another 78-game winning streak — with only one intervening loss — the Grads clearly merited media attention and star status.[14] Fans from districts within driving distance travelled to the Edmonton Arena to see the Grads play, and the Grads games were consistently broadcast over the radio and written up in the newspapers.[15] They became so popular that "...occupants of the best rush seats sat for two hours before the games started and the best reserved seats sold for $1.00 and $1.25 at the big international games held before packed galleries."[16] On May 5, 1930, there were 6,792 spectators at a Grads' home game in the Civic Arena, a crowd that broke all previous records for attendance at any Edmonton sporting event.[17] In an attempt to pay back this generous fan support, the Grads travelled to the outlying towns each year to put on exhibition matches for the residents.[18]

"Grad-appeal" was the domain of the local fans and writers around the country. While the local papers regularly published the statistics of the Grads' games, they also dedicated space on the society pages for the activities of the players themselves.[19] Another measure of the Grads' fame can be found in the fact that local writers such as Frederick B. (Ted) Watt and Franklin Robert Fowler McKitrick dedicated themselves to the task of becoming the Grads' bards. They published numerous literarily doubtful — but heartfelt — Grad-inspired lyrics (see Appendix A). Eastern and American writers seem to have concentrated on the fact that the Grads were a women's team: an amazingly good women's team. An article in the Toronto *Star Weekly* in 1926 effectively sums up the male writer's reactions:

> When you (a male) are persuaded to attend one of these new women's sport functions, you go well fortified with manly condescension. You are prepared to appear amazed. There will, of course, be a good deal of those things that are essentially feminine, such as ineffectual checking and guarding, saving themselves, sparing their tender skin, which, of course, is to be expected. These are girls. Can a leopard forget its spots? These champions do not run like girls. They are lithe, bounding, immeasurably light on their small feet. In three minutes, the old-fashioned man, to mention no names, found it very hard to pay due attention to the charms of the young ladies, as such, owing to the astounding discovery that there was a mighty contest of skill being enacted before his eyes. These champions apparently do not depend upon the skin you love to touch for their success in life. They check cleanly, solidly. They get scratched, bruised, sprained. For the fact of the matter is, unquestionably, that the girls are athletes of the very first rank, that their comprehension of the sport is quite as complete as that of any male team of any description, and the grace with which they do it is utterly and forever beyond the power of males.[20]

Sports writers and fans were not alone in their appreciation of the Grads. Dr. Forrest Allen, who had refereed the Grads' games while they were in Oklahoma, commended Page on his team:

> I have seen college teams composed of men that would have to hustle to take their (the Grads) measure. Gentility in their play and manners both on and off the field made this super-Canadian team an outstanding conviction for the highest type of womanly strength and charm.[21]

The highest compliment of all was presented to the team by Dr. James Naismith, the inventor of basketball:

> My admiration and respect go to you also because you have remained unspoiled by your success, and have retained the womanly graces notwithstanding your participation in a strenu-

ous game. You are not only an inspiration to basketball players throughout the world, but a model for all girls' teams. Your attitude and success have been a source of gratification to me in illustrating the possibilities of the game in the development of the highest type of womanhood.[22]

Winning teams are expected to keep winning, and the Grads did win until they disbanded in 1940. Ironically, their immense ability proved to be an element of their demise. The Grads were so predictable that fans began to attend only the first home games of a series, which caused box-office receipts to drop in the late 1930s. As previously mentioned, the team was still dependent on box-office receipts to supply its travel budget; consequently, this posed problems for the future. Another important factor in the team's demise was J. Percy Page's decision to step down as coach in order to free himself for more active involvement in politics. The deciding factor, however, was the onset of World War II. War not only placed restrictions on travel, but also caused the Grads to lose their playing venue: the Edmonton Arena was commandeered by the Royal Canadian Air Force. The team was finally disbanded on October 14, 1940.[23]

The recognition that the Edmonton Commercial Grads have received since they disbanded has been, on the whole, defined by their statistical achievements. Noel MacDonald (Robertson), the team's captain during the 1930s, was named Canada's woman athlete of the year in 1938, and entered the Canadian Hall of Fame in 1971. In 1973, the Grads were admitted to the Edmonton Hall of Fame. Their admission to the Alberta Sports Hall of Fame followed in 1974.[24] Finally, in 1983, they were inducted into the Canadian Basketball Hall of Fame.[25] The Grads' most recent recognition has come in the form of an award-winning National Film Board tribute, "Shooting Stars," which premiered in Edmonton in 1987.[26] Although this list appears to be impressive, the dearth of serious analytical material dealing with the Grads has resulted in general ignorance, both at the public and academic levels. In order to salvage the achievements of this world-famous, Edmonton-based team, scholars from a number of different disciplines should be prompted to examine the Grads' experience.

II

Why is the Grads' experience important to a women's historian? It is important because it emphasizes the need for women's historians to attempt to reintegrate women into the past, and not to attempt to explain their experience through the limiting, Whiggish tool of feminist history. According to philosophers Jaggar and Struhl (1978), all feminist models contain two fundamental concepts: "...a description of women's oppression, and a prescription for eliminating it."[27] Thus, the basis for all of women's experiences is oppression. Since feminist history is based on one of the four feminist models (Liberalism, Marxism, Radicalism, or Socialism), it concentrates on

Edmonton Commercial Graduates Basketball Club. World's Champions, 1928. Credit: Provincial Archives of Alberta: Photograph Collection A11419.

women's oppression and the chronological process underlying the liberation of women. Historians using this approach examine the past by focusing on the constraining and restrictive sex roles that define women's experience in a patriarchy. Single-minded emphasis on the negative influences present in the female experience by feminist historians presents a skewed vision of women in society.[28] The vast majority of women are members of their own society, not guerillas fighting a battle from within its confines. The feminist tendency to concentrate on the few women who fought against the system or lived outside of its confines yields a "Great Woman" approach to women's history. While this is legitimate, it does not provide a complete understanding of women's experience. It also increases the danger of applying modern values to the study of the past, which is a major pitfall in the feminist approach.

Integrationist history, as it is used in this paper, is an historical approach to the study of women's history that attempts to place women into society and reintegrate them as functioning historical actors. It accepts the idea that sex roles which are currently considered chauvinistic and discriminatory may not have been perceived in that way in other time periods. By examining the society without aiming specifically at finding the roots of women's liberation, or conversely the roots of women's degradation, historians draw their conclusions from their evidence.

Historical and sociological examinations of women in sport are prone to fall into the feminist trap. This is largely due to the traditional interpretation of sport as an inherently masculine, heroic activity. This view posits that sport provides men with a modern rite of passage, as "...the idealized values invested in sport symbolically and socially have important masculine connotations."[29] The values that are idealized in sport are those which western society has defined as peculiarly male: "the tendency toward association, characteristically reserved for men; the opportunity to aggress and prove self, believed to be inherently male instincts; and the demand for perseverance and comparison, elements of male assertiveness."[30] This intertwining of masculinity and sport often leads academics to assume that women and sport are, by definition, culturally incompatible. Hence, women's participation in sport is presumed to lead inevitably to role conflict. When this presupposition is accepted as valid, a feminist approach to the study of women in sport becomes the only logical method of analysis. While there can be no doubt that women's sports' participation has borne the brunt of discrimination throughout history, modern sociological research by Hall, Boutilier, and San Giovanni has found that women do not normally find athletics and femaleness to be mutually exclusive.[31]

A study of the Grads' experience from a strictly feminist perspective would concentrate heavily on the chauvinistic and condescending attitudes prevalent in the male-produced archival sources. Although these attitudes exist, they do not present a complete picture of the Grads' experience. Interviews with the women themselves provide a very different picture of life in pre-World War II society. The fact that the Grads' are a twentieth-century phenomenon, and the players are still alive and willing to provide interviews, makes the women's experience doubly significant. On the one hand, it allows for a more complete understanding of the Grads and their society; on the other hand, the dichotomy in attitudes presented by the print sources and the women's own reminiscences can be used to indicate some of the limitations present in women's history. While it is impossible to change the type of source material available from earlier historical periods, it is important to realize that this information may not be as closely correlated to women's actual experience as imagined. The differences between feminist and integrationist historical approaches, as well as that between male- and female-produced source material, may be explored through a study of four specific areas of the Grads' experience: the reasons underlying the lack of reference to the Grads in academic or athletic texts; the relationship between the concepts of "lady" and "athlete;" the understanding of women's place in their society; and finally, the importance attached to societal myths regarding women and sport.

In order to supplement the printed material pertaining to the Grads, as well as to blanket the period of their greatest popularity, interviews were held with Abbie Scott (Kennedy), 1922-24; Noella 'Babe' Belanger (MacLean), 1929-1937; Edith Stone (Sutton), 1930-34; Evelyn Caulson (Cameron);

Winnie Gallen (Reid) 1936-37/1939-40; and Betty Bawden (Bowen), 1939-40. The number of interviews helped to achieve a consensus of opinion and to lessen the problems inherent in the use of interviews as historical documents; namely, the tendency of memories to become blurred, exaggerated, trivialized, or sentimentalized with time.

The Edmonton Commercial Graduates Basketball Team created one of the most spectacular records in the history of team sports. Aside from newspaper clippings and a few minor magazine articles, however, there is very little printed examination of the Grads' contribution to sport or history. Feminist historians would automatically indicate that this results from the fact that the Grads were a women's team, and as such, they were perceived to be of significantly less importance athletically and historically than men's teams. While it is certainly true that women's athletic prowess and historical contributions have been denigrated simply because they are women's, this explanation cannot be accepted unquestioningly. When the Grads who were interviewed were asked to provide a reason for the lack of printed material, their answers not only included the traditional feminist perspective,[32] but also added other perceptive cultural explanations. Although they did recognize the fact that their status as a women's team was a strike against them[33] they also felt that their western Canadian[34] origins posed an equal problem. The realization that their reign came at a time when both athletic and women's achievements were not accorded the analysis that they are today, and that the team disbanded under the combined strain of Depression and World War II,[35] must be added to the other evidence in order to create a complete picture. The feminist approach becomes limited and incomplete when viewed in this light. A combination of feminist and sociocultural reasons provides a more satisfying and realistic approach to the problem.

The contrast between the way in which the press viewed the Grads as women and as athletes, and the way in which the Grads viewed themselves, is indicative of the polarity that exists between the feminist and integrationist approach to the concepts of "lady" and "athlete." Newspaper and magazine articles which discussed the Grads in other than statistical terms tended to be written by males. These articles, if viewed as the sole examples of original data, provide excellent grist for the feminist mill, as they are extremely chauvinistic by modern standards. Once they are examined in combination with the Grads' own interpretations, however, their chauvinistic stance becomes less important. The apparent polarity between "lady" and "athlete" seems to have bothered many writers, for the majority of the articles dealing with the Grads touch upon these concepts either directly or implicitly. Girls — for that is the appellation given to the female players even though they were all working women — were expected to be ineffectual and poorly disciplined players who would protect themselves from being hurt rather than play aggressively, and whose physical skill level would be far inferior to that of men.[36] They were expected to be far more interested in "...dates, dances, bridge, theatre, and bowling engagements.."[37] than in active participation in a strenuous sport. The athletic woman of 1915 was pictured as a thoroughly unappealing and unladylike figure: "...that strident, belligerent Amazon whom the militant suffragette atrociously exemplifies."[38]

From the very beginning, the Grads amazed writers by being capable athletes. As they gained popularity, they also came to represent the highest ideals of womanhood. The Grads were physically capable of playing a demanding game like basketball, and early writers were awed by this:

> The writer has a very distinct recollection of the day when a girls' basketball game was sort of a travesty, a burlesque of the sport. In those days, girls were booked to play preliminary to a boys' game, just an attraction to keep the crowd amused until the big game went on. The girls did just that thing, and no more, for from start to finish the crowd was in an uproar of laughter.[39]

By 1927, this attitude had been modified somewhat, although writers still appeared to find the idea of aggressive athletic women somewhat threatening:

> Ten bob-haired girls checked their powder puffs and maidenly manners in the dressing room. Folks who went to see a ladylike struggle fainted in the first quarter. If any of those girls gets peeved at her husband, the odds are 10 to 1 he'll wake up in a hospital, and 5 to 1 that he'll spend the rest of his life on crutches.[40]

In 1935, however, this attitude changed to awe, just as the athletes changed into ladies:

> ...now the girls are doing the playing and the men are doing the paying to see them do it: in the place of arousing laughter at their inexpert performances, the young ladies are becoming so proficient that the smug smirks of the male spectators are being replaced by raised eyebrows and open mouths.[41]

Dr. James Naismith summed up public opinion of the Grads when he referred to them as "...a model for all girls' teams..." and "...the development of the highest type of womanhood," in his previously mentioned letter to Dr. Page.

The gap between "lady" and "athlete," as presented in the popular press seems to indicate that times changed very slowly, and that women who were athletes must have endured a great deal of role conflict. Feminist sociologists and historians often focus on the differing expectations that were supposedly placed on women — as women and female athletes — but this falsely presumes that the two can be split up and viewed separately.[42] The simple fact that the concepts of "lady" and "athlete" could be combined has only recently begun to be considered by sociologists, yet it is significant to note

"The Father of Basketball" speaks---

UNIVERSITY OF KANSAS
LAWRENCE

DIVISION OF PHYSICAL EDUCATION
AND
INTERCOLLEGIATE ATHLETICS

Lawrence, July 8, 1925

Mr. J. P. Page,
Edmonton, Canada.

Dear Mr. Page:

It was a distinct pleasure for me to see your team play in Guthrie against the Redbirds. On looking over your girls' record in Canada, the United States and in Europe, I was prepared to see a superior brand of play, but I never expected to see such skill as they demonstrated upon this occasion.

In 1892, at the request of a group of teachers, I organized two girls' basketball teams playing the boys' game, and I found that, due to their lack of experience in athletic contests, the reaction of the girls to the game was vastly different from that of the boys. I was particularly anxious, therefore, to see how the boys' style of game affected the social attributes and the general health of your players, and I can assure you that it was with no little pleasure that I found these young ladies exhibiting as much grace and poise at an afternoon tea as vigorous ability on the basketball court. I can only conclude that this is due very largely to the fine womanly influence of Mrs. Page, supporting your own high standards of sportsmanship and coaching ability.

I feel sure that under proper management, and dominated with right ideals, basketball may be an efficient aid in developing in young women health, skill and refinement, and I would like to congratulate you and your team on the fact that while retaining their fine womanly instincts they have been able to achieve such marked success. I shall always remember your team as a group of young ladies enjoying their sport in a spirit of genuine interest and enthusiasm.

Most sincerely yours,

Jas - Naismith

Dr. James Naismith, of Kansas University, is known wherever basketball is played, as the inventor of the game. Through the courtesy of the Lions' Club, of Guthrie, Okla., Dr. Naismith saw the "Grads" play a championship game in that city. His impressions of the team are given in the above letter.

Letter to J. Percy Page, coach of the Edmonton Commercial Graduates Basketball team, from Dr. James Naismith, University of Kansas, inventor of the game, 1925. Credit: Provincial Archives of Alberta: Photograph Collection A11417.

that this combination is exactly what was expected of the Edmonton Grads. Noel MacDonald (Robertson) explains J. Percy Page's comprehension of this combination as, "Mr. Page insisted that we be ladies first and basketball players second."[43] According to the Grads, a "lady" (in Mr. Page's eyes) didn't drink or smoke, neither was she vulgar nor loud. She was polite, respectful, considerate, and discreet. She was to be an example of womanhood for the community. Page's insistence that the players always act as ladies first and athletes second, was expected to transfer to the basketball court in the form of dedicated, sportsmanlike behavior. As a result, the Grads actually experienced very little role conflict. Considering the fact that all of the Grads were extremely athletic women who participated in a number of other physical sports besides basketball, they would have recognized role conflict had it been present in their lives.[44]

Feminist historians who approach the study of women's history as a means of proving that women have been discriminated against over time, would employ contemporary male sports writers' discussion of the Grads and the restraining aspects of ladylike behavior to be part of the submissive, subordinate female image used to keep women in their "place." It is significant to the integrationist historian that the Grads themselves do not have this understanding. In pre-World War II society, the term "lady" did not carry negative connotations, and the Grads accepted the concept as the ultimate pinnacle of womankind. That society designated specific, culturally-accepted sex roles for both men and women: roles which the Grads, as representative members of the society, never felt to be constraining. The expectations that they, as women, would marry and withdraw from both the athletic and work world to become mothers and homemakers was an accepted part of their world. The fact that "it happened to everybody"[45] made it not only acceptable, but expected. Historians who attempt to see beyond the feminist perspective must be aware that this acceptance of women's roles is extremely important in understanding women's cultural roles. In the light of current women's expectations these parameters appear restrictive, yet for the society of the time, they were not.[46] Even today, in light of the perceived liberation of women, the Grads still express satisfaction with their roles as athletes, wives and mothers.[47] As a matter of fact, the Grads who were interviewed believed that prior to World War II, women held a special position in society simply because they were women, and that the move away from this concept of womanhood has cost women both status and respect.[48]

From an integrationist point of view, this lack of role conflict helps to prove the fact that women are not necessarily unhappy in their societies simply because they do not have the nominal freedoms awarded to modern women. If the sex roles are delineated and accepted by the society, the friction is reduced to a minimum and the majority of the populace will be quite content. This interpretation should act as a check valve for women's historians who see the past as one vast black hole of women's subjugation.

Every society breeds its own pervasive societal myths about women. Canadian society prior to World War II was rife with myths concerning women's reactions to physical activity. The idea that women were physically frail creatures whose health depended on inactivity stemmed from the mistaken Victorian belief that women's biological functions ruled their existence. Women who were physically active were presumed to be in danger of becoming barren — or being able to bear only female children at best. Although any belief that permeates a society has an insidious quality, the Grads' experience indicates that women do not necessarily accept myths simply because they are pervasive. All of the Grads interviewed indicated that they had been cognizant of the myth while they were active team members, but that they had interpreted it as an anachronistic superstition and, consequently, not worthy of note. Edith Sutton was the only Grad whose family used the belief to oppose her athletic participation, yet even she recalls discounting the myth as illogical.[49] The strongest argument against the efficacy of the myth is the continuing existence not only of the Grads Basketball Team but also of all other organized women's sporting activities. Obviously, the myth did not form an active part in women's decision-making processes. It did, however, carry enough societal weight to compel J. Percy Page to refute it publicly in a 1935 newspaper article: "...scores of girls have played under my direction, and while nearly all of these girls have since married, only one has not become a mother."[50] Twenty years later, the myth re-emerged in another *Edmonton Journal* article referring to the sex ratio of the Grads' children: "Boys Win 27 to 25, in Family Score of Grads, Now Proud Wives, Mothers."[51] In spite of the fact that the women who were participating in the sport had ignored the myth's existence, its existence over a twenty-year period is indicative of its strength.

The Edmonton Commercial Graduates thus provide an excellent test case for integrationist historians, because the team was beginning to fade into obscurity and also because their twentieth-century existence allows historians to supplement the male-created print sources with the sentiments and understanding of the women themselves. Between 1915 and 1940, the Grads provided Alberta and the world with the best basketball it had ever seen. As women, the Grads' experience shows that the limited feminist approach to historical survey is not sufficient to completely explain women's experience. The team's tendency to slip towards obscurity can be explained only partially because the Grads were a women's team; additional factors that affected the team's longevity included its western and Canadian origins, and the tenor of the time. Similarly, the concepts of "lady" and "athlete" cannot be fully explained from a feminist perspective, for the feminist interpretation tends to equate "lady" with negative connotations, and can only perceive the two concepts as mutually exclusive.

Women's ability to disregard or discount those societal myths which seem to be out of step with the time is an indication of women's ability to cope with society through the use of logic and common sense, two traits which have little historical press. The Grads' experience shows that women were not only able to live with the concept of womanhood that was present in Alberta prior to World War II, but that they actually feel women have lost a sense of respect and uniqueness through women's liberation. The integrationist approach to women's history allows historians to explore women's experience without attempting to force it into a pre-formed mold. This attempt to reintegrate women into history and society must continue if historians wish to readjust the imbalances created by both traditional and feminist historical approaches to the history of women.

APPENDIX A

TRIBUTE TO THE GRADS — FREDERICK B. WATT
(Provincial Archives of Alberta. Access –70.27/5)

No broken army in retreat,
    No loafers, through success gone soft,
But lithe and firm upon their feet
    They leave the field with flags aloft.
The game is played, the records stand —
    The brightest team that ever shone
Has heard "Dismiss!" But o'er the land
    The spirit of The Gang sweeps on.

Forever changing, yet unchanged,
    Tradition linking year by year,
They met the best the world could range —
    The best that brought no lasting peer.
Yet if the secret's to be found
    In human hearts, 'tis wise to look;
That perfect system isn't bound
    Between the covers of a book.

They brought their city more than fame,
    They brought their nation more than pride;
The strongest foe, the toughest game
    Were things they simply took in stride.
For first they faced the inward jars —
    The jealousy, the selfish dreams'
These things that make outstanding stars
    But wreck consistent, winning teams.

The pass that meant another's score,
    The faith that fed another's drive
Were constant on and off the floor,
    For every year of twenty-five.

* * *

Today we face a greater game;
    For life and freedom must we play,
And we shall need the gallant flame
    The "Grads" have lit along the way.

NOTES

1. _____,"Introduction," *Edmonton Grads 25 Years of Basketball Championships*, (Royal Bank publications, 1975) p. 1.
2. *Ibid.* p. 2.
3. Unpublished personal interviews, Babe Belanger MacLean, Feb. 25, 1988. Winnie Gallen Reid, Feb. 25, 1988. Betty Bawden Bowen, Feb. 25, 1988. Edith Stone Sutton, Feb. 26, 1988. Evelyn Cameron, Feb. 28, 1988. Abbie Scott Kennedy, Feb. 28, 1988.
4. *Ibid.*
5. Reid/MacLean/Bowen interviews.
6. *25 Years*, p. 16.
7. Interviews/*25 Years*, p. 3.
8. *Ibid.*
9. *25 Years*, p. 4.
10. *Ibid.*
11. *Ibid.*
12. Reid interview.
13. *25 Years*, p. 15.
14. *25 Years*, p. 1.
15. MacLean/Kennedy interviews.
16. Franklin Robert Fowler McKitrick, Personal Papers, The Provincial Archives of Alberta, Access –72.226.
17. *25 Years*, p. 5.
18. MacLean/Kennedy/Cameron interviews.
19. "Shooting Stars," *National Film Board*, 1987.
20. _____, "Bobbed-Headed Athletes Menace Male Supremacy," *The Toronto Star Weekly*, April 24, 1926. In The Provincial Archives of Alberta. Access –70.27/5.
21. Letter from Dr. Forrest Allen to Dr. J. Percy Page. July 8, 1925. The Provincial Archives of Alberta. Access –70.27/61.
22. _____, *Sitting on Top of the World*. Grads Commemorative Booklet. Provincial Archives of Alberta. Access –70.17/176.
23. *25 Years*, p. 5.
24. *Ibid.*
25. Bowen interview.
26. "Shooting Stars."
27. As cited in Mary A. Boutilier and Lucinda SanGiovanni, *The Sporting Woman*, (Champaign: Human Kinetics, 1983), p. 12.
28. See Ellen W. Gerber, "Historical Survey," in *The American Woman in Sport*, Ellen Gerber et.al. eds., (Don Mills: Addison-Wesley, 1974), pp. 3-47. This representative feminist history examines the feminine ideals with relation to sport and concentrates on the negative aspects of women's experience. In order to support this view, the author depends heavily on the writings of early twentieth-century educators and medical men. She summarizes their objections to women's participation in athletics:

    Sport requires vigor; the ideal required delicacy. Sport takes one out of the home and into the tempting, defiling world. Sport places participants in positions where their flesh is exposed and their emotions are expressed; the ideal requires modesty, propriety, and circumspectness. Furthermore, by exposing the face and the reproductive organs to possible injury, sport endangers the ultimate Victorian goal: the twin functions of attracting a man and bearing a child.

    Unfortunately, she does not explain women's actual participation in sport as satisfactorily.
29. Jan Felshin, "The Dialectic of Woman and Sport," in *The American Woman in Sport*, Ellen Gerber, et. al. eds., (Don Mills: Addison-Wesley, 1974), p. 182.
30. *Ibid.* p.184.

31. M. Ann Hall, *Sport, Sex Roles and Sex Identity.* (CRIAW: Ottawa, 1981). See also Boutilier.
32. Sutton/Reid interviews.
33. Bowen/Sutton/Reid interviews.
34. Kennedy/Reid/Bowen/Sutton interviews.
35. Bowen/MacLean/Cameron interviews.
36. *Star Weekly*/Scrapbook, Provincial Archives of Alberta. Access -70.27/5.
37. Don Murray, "My Basketball Musings," *Sports Review.* (May 1932): 15. In Provincial Archives of Alberta. Access -70.27/5.
38. Adrian J. Brenner, "The Girls Take the Floor," *Converse Basketball Yearbook*, 1930. Provincial Archives of Alberta. Access -70.27/5.
39. Don Maxwell, "Girls War Like Amazons on Basketball Floor," newspaper clipping 1927.n.p. In Grad's personal archives.
40. *Canadian Magazine.*
41. *Hall*, p. 13.
42. _____, "*Wonder Team*," Magazine Clipping. n.p., n.d., Provincial Archives of Alberta. Access -70.27/11.
43. Personal interviews.
44. Cameron interview.
45. Sutton interview.
46. Personal interviews.
47. Reid/Bowen/MacLean interviews.
48. Personal interviews. *passim.*
49. *Canadian Magazine.*
50. Grads' personal archives.

BIBLIOGRAPHY

There were a number of problems in researching this paper. Archival sources were badly documented, if they were documented at all; consequently, in many cases I have not been able to pinpoint either the time or place of publications. In order to ease matters, the bibliographic references will be made to the major collections that were used, while the footnotes make reference to the specific selections in these collections which are pertinent. The personal interviews were conducted in the homes of the Grads.

Boutilier, Mary A. and Lucinda San Giovanni. *The Sporting Woman.* Champaign: Human Kinetics, 1983.

Bowen, Betty. Personal Interview. Feb. 25, 1988.

Cameron, Evelyn. Personal Interview. Feb. 28, 1988.

Davidson, Sue. ed. *Out of the Bleachers.* New York: Feminist Press, 1979.

Edmonton Commercial Grads' Private Archives. Betty Bowen.

_____, *Edmonton Grads 25 Years of Basketball Championships*, Royal Bank publication, 1975.

Gerber, Ellen W. *et. al.* eds. *The American Woman in Sport.* Don Mills: Addison-Wesley, 1974.

Hall, M. Ann. *Sport, Sex Roles and Sex Identity.* CRIAW: Ottawa, 1981.

Kennedy, Abbie. Personal Interview. Feb. 28, 1988.

MacLean, Noella "Babe." Personal Interview. Feb. 25, 1988.

McKitrick, Franklin Robert Fowler. Personal Papers. Provincial Archives of Alberta. Access -72.226.

Provincial Archives of Alberta. Access –70.27/1, 70.27/2, 70.27/3, 70.27/4, 70.27/5, 70.27/6, 70.27/7, 70.27/8, 70.27/9, 70.27/11, 70.27/58, 70.27/59, 70.27/60a, 70.27/61, 70.27/176.

Reid, Winnie. Personal Interview. Feb. 25, 1988.

"Shooting Stars," *National Film Board.* 1988.

Sutton, Edith. Personal Interview. Feb. 26, 1988.

MAKING BANFF A YEAR-ROUND PARK

W. B. Yeo

A winter visitor to Banff National Park might meet the occasional snow-shoer, and in the town it is possible to while away the season at the curling or hockey rinks. But the big winter sport is skiing. Although the park provides opportunities for all kinds of skiing, the crowds are to be found on the slopes at the three major downhill ski areas.

It has been over ninety years since the first skis showed up in Banff, during which time the number of skiers has grown from less than a half dozen to hundreds of thousands every year. The nature of the sport has changed as well. In the beginning, the organization of ski events and expeditions was in the hands of amateur organizations, while the equipment and techniques meant that the enjoyment of the sport depended more on effort and skill than on machinery. Today the crowds line up to ride sophisticated lifts to the top of their favourite groomed slope, to ski perhaps on artificial snow, all provided at a price by a commercial ski-area operator.

The growth and change of Banff National Park's ski areas has been more spasmodic than dramatic. When compared with other sites where the alpine ski industry has flowered, it is often said that Norquay, Sunshine and Lake Louise are country cousins, lacking the latest amenities and showing obvious signs of a difficult and deprived childhood. All too often these conditions are blamed on the restrictions imposed by the park authorities. However, the history of skiing and winter sports in general in Banff National Park shows that the authorities rarely resisted new initiatives, although they did attempt to contain change within the scope of policy and regulations. On the other hand, the proponents of development, with the possible exception of Sir Norman Watson, seldom looked beyond the range of their limited capital.

The need for long-term planning for ski areas became critical when major technological changes were introduced into downhill skiing. This factor initiated a snowball effect, where investment in machinery meant that additional investment in other amenities was called for to attract and hold the visitors, who would then pay for the original investment. This snowball is now rolling downhill at a faster rate than ever, and the old official method of dealing with ski-hill development proposals on an incremental basis cannot cope with it. Challenges to park management today are a far cry from the simpler days when it all began with the Banff Winter Carnival.

At the turn of the century, Banff was like any other small one-industry town in western Canada when it came to making the best of winter. With most of Rocky Mountains Park virtually shut down for the cold months, the permanent population in the townsite turned to curling and hockey, and to tobogganing — a sport in which Banff enjoyed certain natural advantages over communities on the prairie.[1]

The more prosperous residents were migratory, and fled to the coast for the winter. Banff used to be a quiet place after September, certainly up to fairly recent times. Local oral tradition speaks of several off-season pastimes, including those adopted by the less energetic townspeople. For businessmen whose enterprises did not close for the winter, or whose purses did not permit an escape to warmer climates, there was the daily round of visits to back offices, where the desk often concealed a jug of rye.

It may have been at one of these late-morning gatherings that someone complained of things being too quiet in the winter, and perhaps they should do something about it. There may have been dissenters present who retorted that they liked it that way, but the notion of somehow luring paying visitors to the town had its appeal. If their livelier fellow Banffites could have fun in the snow and on the ice, so could outsiders.

Typically the Canadian Pacific Railway took the lead, and in 1910 the company turned its extensive advertising effort toward promoting Banff as a year-round resort. Its Banff Springs Hotel had recently been expanded and modernized, providing an opportunity to expand its business beyond the hectic summer months. However, this effort failed, and it fell to prominent local men to find a way of attracting winter visitors. In the summer of 1916 the idea of a Banff Winter Carnival was born. After several months of uphill campaigning the Festival opened on February 5, 1917.[2]

Winter carnivals had been a familiar feature in many parts of Canada for a generation or more. One ingredient had become standard fare at such events, and that was the ice palace. Banff's first Carnival had a big one. The organizers managed to have it built by internees from the nearby winter camp at the Cave and Basin. These men were mainly eastern Europeans who had migrated from the Austro-Hungarian Empire, which, in 1917, made them enemy aliens. They were rounded up and sent to camps partly because most of them had been thrown out of work in 1914 when the war began. They were a potential charge on local communities so internment was a handy alternative to paying relief. The men sent to Rocky Mountains Park spent the summer at a camp near Castle Mountain, but in winter they moved closer to town, and had to be kept busy. There is no known record of what the aliens thought of building a palace out of ice.

In any case, the ice palace was a success, and despite the absence of free

Banff Avenue during the Winter Carnival in 1929.
Credit: The Whyte Museum of the Canadian Rockies.

Ski Party in Banff National Park, 1920's.
Credit: The Whyte Museum of the Canadian Rockies

labour after the war, such displays became a regular part of subsequent Carnivals. In addition, there were ice sculptures and Indian tipis along Banff Avenue, the latter being a reminder of the Banff Indian Days that had been running every summer for several years. The ice palace, however, was the focal point for the many sporting events that took place during the Carnival.

The events included a wide variety of winter sports. For many years the Banff Curling Club organized gala bonspiels and invited rinks from other parts of Alberta to participate. There were snowshoe and cross-country ski races. By 1920 skijoring (in which the skier is pulled by a horse) was included. But right from the start, the feature attraction in the early years of the Carnival was always ski jumping.

Skiing and ski jumping were not new to Banff in 1917. The first known set of skis to appear there were sent to George Paris in the winter of 1894, by a Norwegian-American visitor. In 1910 the great mountain guide, Conrad Kain, arrived with a pair of Norwegian Telemark skis, and these were quickly copied by Captain Jack Stanley at his Minnewanka lumber and boat works. In the winter of 1911, residents of the town went ski touring in near-by valleys. A small ski jump was set up on Tunnel Mountain, where several Banff youngsters were introduced to that sport. With Kain's departure, there was a decline in activity, but the advent of the Winter Carnival put a new spark into local skiing.

Although the young locals were eager to participate, the first Carnival skiing events were dominated by outsiders, particularly by entrants from Revelstoke and Camrose who represented Norwegian sports clubs. One of these, Gus Johnson, stayed in Banff after the first Carnival, and became the nucleus of a group of local enthusiasts who formed the Banff Ski Club.

As the ski-jumping event at the Winter Carnival grew over the years, it became part of the North American professional circuit. The lesser mortals of the local ski fraternity were frequently relegated to Class B and C levels of the event. Class A was reserved for the professionals. As it is today, ski jumping for most people was a spectator sport. It is not surprising that the more restless souls began to seek other opportunities such as competitive slalom racing, or the thrill of the long run in some as yet undiscovered deep powder country.

Nineteen-thirty was a big year for amateur skiing in Banff National Park. In that year Cliff White was elected president of the Banff Ski Club, and he initiated a competitive ski development program that led to slalom racing on the slopes of Mount Norquay.[3] In the same year, Skoki Lodge was built in an area accessible from Lake Louise station, following an extensive recon-naisance by White and Cyril Paris. Permission to build was denied at first until White and Paris resubmitted their application as representatives of the "Mount Norquay Ski Club." Even then, the success of the venture depended upon the intervention of Peter and Catherine Whyte, who leased the facility, and operated it during its early years.[4]

The growth of skiing in the Park reached a pinnacle in 1937 when the

Ski Jump, Banff National Park, 1920's.
Credit: The Whyte Museum of the Canadian Rockies

Boy with skis in Banff National Park, 1920's.
Credit: The Whyte Museum of the Canadian Rockies

Dominion Ski Championships of the Canadian Amateur Ski Association were held in Banff. The development of the sport in western Canada had received major recognition, which led the Canadian Pacific Railway to introduce the first of its western snow-train excursions.

The 1937 competitions, followed by those of subsequent years, were held at Mount Norquay. The 300-foot run laid out years before by Gus Johnson had been improved considerably. A lodge built in 1928 burned down in 1937, but was replaced two years later. A key development was the building of an access road up the slopes of adjoining Stoney Squaw Mountain. This project depended on special government funding as an employment project for relief workers. The earlier Class A ski jump on Tunnel Mountain was removed to make way for highway improvements, and replaced as a Park project by a new jump on Mount Norquay in 1936. In 1941, Mount Norquay entered the mechanical age when a rope tow was installed.

Until the end of the Second World War the development of the Mount Norquay Ski Area was supervised by an amateur ski club with the co-operation of Park authorities. At this point, the assets were assumed by Banff Chairlift Corporation Ltd., solely owned by George Encil, who had European ski-area experience. In exchange, Encil undertook the financing of major improvements, including the introduction of a chairlift.[11] Encil sold the operation in 1960, and through the efforts of a succession of owners, there has been a continual upgrading of the site's facilities. The current owners are considering further expansion of their operation, but there are serious constraints arising from the nature of the site.[5]

The Ptarmigan Valley area, opened up for ski touring by Clifford White and Cyril Paris, attracted the attention of Sir Norman Watson, a British industrialist with a passion for deep-powder snow. He knew the ski areas of Switzerland and Austria intimately, and saw in the Canadian Rockies an opportunity for creating a new mecca for Alpine skiers. Skoki Lodge had since been joined by Temple Lodge and Halfway Hut to form a network of ski trails with ready connection to Lake Louise. Temple became popular for downhill skiing, although there was no lift. These assets were managed by a new club organized by White, The Ski Club of the Canadian Rockies, which also assumed control of Mount Norquay. The Club was incorporated, and control shifted to Watson who attempted to attract capital and official sanction for a major development. His scheme included the settlement in the valley of refugee Austrian ski guides, a lease granting exclusive control over a large land area, and the construction of an access road and six "chalet hotels."

The outbreak of World War II meant very little was done to implement Watson's scheme, and it was not until the early 1950's that a shift in interest from ski touring to downhill skiing led to the installation of a rope tow at Temple. The Ski Club of the Canadian Rockies Ltd. formed a subsidiary, Lake Louise Lifts, to construct a sight-seeing gondola on the south face of Whitehorn Mountain. This development was encouraged by the govern-

"Snowshoe Tramp" in Banff National Park, 1920's.
Credit: The Whyte Museum of the Canadian Rockies

ment, and led to the cutting of higher ski runs and the introduction of new lift equipment, new trails, and new lodges. Artificial snow-making equipment has recently been installed. This ski area is now known as Lake Louise, and receives over 400,000 ski visits per season.

As a ski area, Sunshine had a slightly different origin from that of Mount Norquay and Lake Louise, in that commercial operators were in charge from the beginning, rather than amateur clubs. J. E. Brewster of Banff took over the operation of the CPR rest house at Sunshine (built for summer use in 1928), and in 1934 he began ski excursions there. This enterprise continued to grow through the war years, particularly after the site became accessible by road from Banff, because its snow season was so much longer than Mount Norquay's. The Brewsters could also offer overnight accommodation. The growth of this facility was achieved through expansion of the original cabin and considerable sleight-of-hand as far as official permission was concerned. A temporary rope tow was added in 1942, and replaced by a permanent one three years later.[7]

In 1952, George Encil acquired the Sunshine operation and made substantial improvements, but it was after Cliff and Bev White took over in 1960 that major changes in accommodation and lift technology were introduced. The Whites attracted outside capital by selling part interest to a large corporation, beginning a series of ownership changes leading up to 1981. Developments and expansion have been almost continuous. In 1941 the Brewsters had built a road to allow skiers to be brought from the Mount Royal Hotel in Banff directly to Sunshine. These bus rides were famous social affairs, but the tradition ended in 1980 when a large gondola lift was built directly to the ski area from a lower parking lot. In recent years, Sunshine has played host to a number of competitive downhill races, thereby attracting considerable international attention.

Today, the fully modern ski area in Europe or North America is a capital-intensive development. Large investments are made in the latest and fastest lift equipment, in snow-making apparatus, and in roads and buildings. Frequently there are substantial modifications to the ski terrain itself. In fact, many ski areas are visitor destinations in themselves, providing a self-contained world where accommodation and "apres-ski" entertainment complement the actual ski facilities. The grandfather of all such places in North America is Sun Valley, Idaho, which opened in 1936. This site has shown the way for many succeeding developments elsewhere in the Rocky Mountains.[9]

Sun Valley was big right from the start. It was developed by the Harriman interests and the Union Pacific Railroad, so capital was readily available. As described above, the situation in Banff National Park was quite different until recent times, so development of ski areas occurred gradually. Sir Norman Watson foresaw the difficulties of attracting capital and official support for new and seemingly remote sites, despite their technical advantages, so much of his effort prior to the outbreak of war consisted of publicizing his scheme among the wealthy and influential.[10]

Sun Valley has now been eclipsed somewhat by other more spectacular ski areas, and today's model is the so-called "world-class ski resort." The ski areas in Banff National Park may fall short of this status, but many changes have occurred since the days of Gus Johnson and the Banff Ski Club. The long road from homemade skis to hot tubs and gondola lifts is marked by the influence of the Winter Carnival, the work of the early amateur skiers and their clubs, and the transformation of downhill skiing in the Park from a volunteer to a commercial enterprise. The response of officials in the Park and in Ottawa was always cautious, but ultimately supportive of this incremental change.[11]

The commercialization of downhill skiing was directly related to the introduction of expensive technology. This technology came initially in the shape of simple rope tows, but it served to make the sport widely popular.[12] Such innovations, and later improvements such as chair lifts, required capital and management skills. An influx of skiers attracted by new equipment demanded other facilities to accommodate them. These needs were met initially by locally-based entrepreneurs, so that the rate of ski-area development in Banff National Park was limited by their available resources.

It is difficult to state with any certainty how the authorities of the day would have reacted had Sir Norman Watson, or any other promoter, managed to find the means to build a massive Sun Valley type of ski area before the war. They were very conservative when dealing with the incremental proposals that did appear, but did not raise outright opposition. In the 1950's and 1960's there seemed to be official encouragement for large developments (such as the Whitehorn Gondola and the abortive 1972 Lake Louise resort proposal),[13] but no sign of a long-range vision of what the ski areas could, or should become. It is possible that few over the past 60 years, if any, foresaw how skiing would evolve from an amateur pastime into a large-scale commercial enterprise.

Only in recent years have Parks Canada authorities begun to assess the rate of change in the ski areas with a view to predicting and measuring the impact of future development on Banff National Park. No longer is it acceptable to discuss a single new facility or individual management practice in isolation. Long-term development plans are required. Close consultation with ski area operators is a necessary ingredient. Unfortunately the lure of the latest gadgetry gets the better of cool heads, and the ancient practice of bursting through the Superintendent's door with a massive new scheme is still alive; but it's not supposed to work anymore.

The reason for concern about the direction ski areas may be taking comes from a legislated requirement to protect the natural values of the Park, in the face of increasing pressures for larger and more elaborate facilities. While the ski areas themselves are financed by their operators and their backers, the necessary infrastructure to support such a large-scale human activity as downhill skiing is provided by the Park. It would be very unlikely that the authorities could justify direct intervention, as they did in the old pre-commercial days when interned aliens built an ice palace or relief workers cleared the Stoney Squaw road. Nevertheless, the maintenance of access roads, protection from avalanches, and social services for employees are all, or partly, paid for out of the public purse. Ski areas pay land rent, which entitles them to use of Crown land, but they make little direct contribution to externalized infrastructure costs.[14]

The developmental model that the larger ski areas seem to wish to emulate is the "tourist destination," or world-famous self-contained resort. Documents produced by their promoters always refer to this goal as a desirable economic objective that would enhance the regional economy. While this assertion may, or may not, be true, it is certain that self-contained destinations within national parks tend to move away from the legislated purposes for which the parks were originally established. Such destinations could exist anywhere that suitable terrain exists.

As the skiing population ages, the nature of the commercial ski area business is changing. In the United States this phenomenon has led to what one observer has described as the "golfification" of skiing.[15] To "golfify" skiing is to reduce effort and risk, and to increase comfort. Aside from the provision of hot tubs, luxury suites and all-night entertainment, this process frequently involves massive modification of the terrain to smooth out the bumps. In place of the golf cart, there is the high speed "quad chair."

Perhaps the extreme limit of — "golfification" is the possible separation of the "total experience" from the traditional ski-area locale. It is technically possible to ski without snow, or even without a ski hill. In fact, an indoor ski hill is planned in Japan, which would permit the ski area operator to manage the unpredictable parts of his business: the weather and the terrain. Indeed, he could do without weather and terrain, and create his own environment close to his market. Time-consuming and expensive travel to remote mountainous areas would be eliminated.

The scenario of uprooting the ski area, and taking it to the skier is not likely to appeal to those who regard the journey to a snowbound mountain wilderness as a bonus. The greater challenge to individual skill and effort is experienced in a natural setting, but Banff National Park has a legacy of technical enhancements that puts part of that challenge within range of thousands. To some extent that legacy is the result of pioneering work that began early in this century. The question is: how far can we go to reduce the challenge without diminishing the mountain environment? After all, it was the mountain environment that lured Banff's ski pioneers out onto the slopes so many years ago.

NOTES

1. Great Plains Research Consultants, "Banff National Park, 1792-1965: A History;" Canadian Parks Service, *Microfiche Report Series* –196.
2. Lund, Rolf T., "The Development of Skiing in Banff;" *Alberta Historical Review*, Autumn, 1977.
3. Kutschera, Victor, "Development of Skiing at Banff and in the Rockies," 1938; Canadian Parks Service, Western Region, Historical Reference File, "Skiing" (Reference File).
4. McDowall, Hilary, "Ski Runners;" Alice Fulmer Papers, Folder 17, Archives of the Canadian Rockies M70. Also Superintendent, Banff National Park to Commissioner of National Parks, Ottawa, 1 June 1932; Reference File.
5. Crawford, G. L. to Director, National Parks Branch, 4 October 1956; Reference File.
6. Watson, Sir Norman, "The Development of Skiing in the Canadian Rockies;" memorandum dated 1936; Reference File. Also correspondence, Watson to P. J. Jennings (Superintendent Banff National Park), 1936-1939; Reference File.
7. Mills, Edward, "Sunshine Village;" Historic Sites and Monuments Board *Agenda Paper*, 1987.
8. Crawford, G. L., *op. cit.*
9. Watson, Sir Norman, "The Development etc.;" *op. cit.* Also P. J. Jennings to W. H. H. Williamson (Comptroller, National Parks Bureau), 23 August 1938; Reference File.
10. Watson, Sir Norman, to T. A. Crerar (Minister of Mines and Resources), 5 July 1937; and Watson to P. J. Jennings, 14 November 1938; Reference File.
11. Williamson, F. H. H., to Sir Norman Watson, 27 October 1938: "we are in full sympathy with the aims and objects of your organization, and ...we are prepared at all times to facilitate progress within the limits of our legislative powers;" Reference File. Also R. Touche, "The First Fifty Years;" memorandum n.d., file 1, Archives of the Canadian Rockies M377.
12. Crawford, G. L., *op. cit.*
13. Touche, R., *op. cit.*
14. Canadian Parks Service, Western Region.
15. Rademan, Miles C., "Ski Town Prediction: Obstacles Ahead;" *Planning*, February, 1987.

SKIING FOR IDENTITY AND TRADITION:
SCANDINAVIAN VENTURE AND ADVENTURE
IN THE PACIFIC NORTHWEST, 1900-1960

Jorgen Dahlie

"...once again we have given skiing a push forward in northern
B. C. by making these two days the greatest sports days here in
the Cariboo, where mining is our bread, and skiing our soul."[1]

The writer is Kaare Hegseth, a Norwegian immigrant who had settled in
the mining town of Wells a half-century ago. The annual ski tournament of
1936 had just been staged, and a checklist of the competitors — Elvenes,
Hagemoen, Brandvold, Kaldahl, and Holst — reveals an unmistakeably
Norwegian presence. Hegseth himself was not an outstanding skier, but was
zealous in his promotion of the sport. His belief that skiing was something
more than a leisure-time activity was shared by most Scandinavians. As did
many of his countrymen, Hegseth skied for pleasure, but he also spent
untold hours laying out ski trails, preparing jumping hills, and competing
in tournaments throughout the province as finances allowed. This "social
investment" in sporting activities, as one historian has called it, was essentially the maintenance of identity and tradition, an instinctive means of
easing the transition from Old World to New. Skiing was deeply ingrained
in the culture, and in some ways served to condition the response to a new
environment.[2]

In the following discussion, I will amplify the foregoing by looking at the
fortunes of some individuals central to the development of skiing in the
Pacific Northwest. The focus will be primarily on Hegseth's fellow immigrants, both predecessors and contemporaries. Incidentally, his juxtaposi-
tion of mining and skiing — bread and soul — turned out to be more
perceptive than he might have thought. The careers of many Scandinavians
in skiing history were often linked to the particular milieux of western mining
communities. It was true for such turn of the century figures as Olaus
Jeldness, Torgal Noren, and Engwald Engen, as well as for the Brandvold
brothers in the Garibaldi venture. And, in an ironic sense, it held true for

some who left Kongsberg, Norway, specifically to avoid underground work in the silver mines only to find themselves later at Copper Mountain, Caribou Gold Quartz, or Island Mountain in Wells. The so-called "Three Musketeers" of the 1930's — Kaldahl, Mobraaten, and Sotvedt — were a part of that Kongsberg exodus which figured so prominently in the history of this period. In any event, Hegseth would have been aware that the circumstances of unemployment, transiency, and pioneer working conditions of isolated communities dictated to an extent how Scandinavians would take up their traditional winter sports whenever opportunities arose.[3]

From the late 1890's to the First World War, mining booms were a feature of the Kootenays and in certain counties of Washington, Idaho, and Montana. In such localities as Greenwood, Phoenix, and Rossland in the Kootenays, or Ione, Cle Elum, and Spokane south of the 49th, the industry attracted many immigrants. Scandinavians were among those drawn by the prospect of economic gain, but, for the majority, no great fortunes were made. However, the life and times of Olaus Jeldness proved him to be an exception: when his ashes were scattered over Rossland's Red Mountain in 1935, perhaps only a few fellow Scandinavians would have recalled his role in skiing history or why this wealthy Spokane entrepreneur should have chosen Red Mountain for his final exit. A brief account of the Jeldness career suggests that the heritage of skiing and its values ranked equally high with his successful mining ventures.[4]

In an essay entitled "Skiing, the Royal Sport of the Northlands" written in 1909, Jeldness reflected on some of his views of the national pastime in the Old Country: "The skisport is associated with nearly all the folklore of Norway, and like its mountains and fjords, and great water falls, and sagas, it is indelibly stamped on its history. It is being appreciated now in all snow countries, as the manifest and cleanest sport in existence. Skiing is essentially a good fellowship and companionable sport." He went on to contrast skiing with American games in which life and limb are often sacrificed, noting that "...the ski contests stand over them all as a challenge in cleanness, superior individual courage and skill."[5] Such sentiments were not uncommon among his fellow skiers. Aged 53 when he expressed these views, Jeldness had stopped competing, but skied well into the 1930's. Born in Stangvik, Nordmore (south of Trondheim) in 1856, he skied as a youngster, then left Norway in 1873 for the United States. Over the next 25 years he worked in the mines of Michigan, Missouri, South Dakota, and Colorado with an interval in 1882 that took him to Spitsbergen for the Arctic Coal Company of Boston. He arrived in Rossland in 1896, having become wealthy through the promotion and sale of claims.

It was during his sojourn in the Kootenays that Jeldness demonstrated his prowess on skis, dominating a succession of exhibitions and winter carnivals in Rossland from 1896 to 1900. Thereafter, the Jeldness trophies — some of which are now on display in the local museum — were presented for annual competitions in the region. Jeldness captured the Canadian jumping and downhill titles for three years, but his achievements should be viewed in the context of the times. Nevertheless, accounts of his runs from the summit of Red Mountain attest to his daring and ability. Contemporary reports indicate that the spectacle of Jeldness, a long pole held aloft overhead, hurtling down the steep slopes of Red Mountain kept Rossland spectators spellbound.

Jeldness returned to Spokane in 1910. By his showmanship and skill he had laid the foundation for competitive skiing in western Canada. By 1915 Scandinavians had arranged tournaments and formed clubs in Rossland, Greenwood, Phoenix, and Revelstoke. Similar developments took place in Ione, Kingsgate, Cle Elum, and Spokane to the south, while Norwegians primarily had sparked the movement as early as 1910 in Camrose, Edmonton, Calgary, and Banff. The tournament records of the times indicate that an informal network kept Scandinavians apprised of ski meets throughout this large region.[6]

To appreciate the atmosphere of these early tournaments, it is instructive to look at some examples of how the skiers' exploits were recorded. Most accounts were written by observers with little knowledge of the sport, or more concerned with so-called world or national records. What the accounts lacked in understanding or accuracy was more than compensated for by poetic description and lofty prose. The following passage is representative of the narrative style and its effort to capture the moment:

> He climbed up the mountain…and came down at a terrific rate of speed. At the jump off he went higher in the air than ever before, and skimmed along through space with the grace of a flying machine, and landed on the steep slope a long distance down the hill. Many exclamations of great surprise went up from the crowd. The official measurers, Messrs. Renwick and Cruickshanks, announced that he had jumped 103 feet 8 inches, which is the longest jump ever made in Canada.[7]

Torgal Noren of Norway was the performer; over the years he garnered six consecutive jumping and downhill titles, taking possession of one of the Jeldness trophies.[8]

Other reports tell of downhill skiers shooting along courses as if impelled from cannons. At times, as in this description of a cross country race, the detail could be excessive: "The race started at the Bank of Montreal Building, west along Columbia Avenue, below the baseball grounds to White Bear Mine, then following the course marked with flags around Red Mountain, on the Jumbo mine wagon road, thence across Centre Star Gulch at the flag opposite Virginia Mine buildings; up Monte Cristo mountain, keeping to the north side of the flag…"[9]

That particular contest had only three entrants, including Engwald Engen, another Norwegian who succeeded Noren in the then well-established competition for the Jeldness trophy. From the record, it is clear that Jeldness, Noren, and Engen had significant roles to play in the start of competitive skiing: their exploits dramatized for non-Scandinavians the possibilities of the sport for spectators and participants alike. By the time of Nels Nelsen's legendary flights on the Revelstoke hill in the 1920's, skiing had definitely caught the public imagination.[10] How much it had done so was to be under-scored with the emergence of the Kongsberg connection — the stage would now be set for the most eventful chapter in Pacific Northwest ski history.

May 13, 1987, marked the opening in Kongsberg of what one observer called "...the world's most outstanding ski museum..." with its impressive collection of thousands of trophies. For all who follow skiing, the opening was a reminder of the golden era when Kongsberg skiers topped world and Olympic competition from 1928 to 1948. Among those taking part in the ceremonies was Vancouver's Tormod (Tom) Mobraaten, twice a Canadian Olympic competitor who left Kongsberg in 1930. Along with fellow immi-grants Nordal Kaldahl, Henry Sotvedt, Olav Ulland, and Hjalmar Hvam, he came to symbolize the Norwegian factor in virtually every major tour-nament from the 1930's to the post-war period.[11] It was their presence on the jumping hills, cross-country trails, and alpine runs which drew thousands to see skiing at its best — and very often for the first time. It was an era, as the late Henry Sotvedt put it, when "...it was fun in our free time to jump on those primitive jumping hills, built by us as Norwegian immigrants — and to see the Canadians' surprise, interest, and afterwards their growing enthusiasm."[12] The legacy of skiing in the Pacific Northwest was not entirely bequeathed by the Kongsberg five, nor only by Scandinavians for that matter. They did, however, have a very substantial role in defining the extent of that legacy.

A key to understanding the impact of the Scandinavians and the Kongsberg five can be found in the Old Country experience. An explana-tion of what the background meant has been set forth by Norman Berger, himself a three-time champion in the 1920's.

> I can remember when I was a lad in Norway the way we used to train. Gathering after school on a certain hill, we built our own take-off, tramped down the landing, then some of us took two or three jumps while the other boys stood by and criticized us as to take-off and landing. After this kind of practice, we usually went on run across country — the leader trying to find the most difficult descents as well as the most difficult climbs. When you realize that the majority of the competitors very often ski ten or fifteen miles to get to the place where the competition is taking place, then ski the same distance home, ...you can readily understand that skiing becomes second nature to these boys...[13]

Recent conversations with Ulland, Hvam, and Mobraaten confirmed what Berger had to say. Mobraaten stressed that such free time activity was what they looked forward to doing; the discipline fostered by having to make do on their own shaped in large measure their attitude toward competition. Incidentally, the kind of varied practices described by Berger explains why the skiers became skilled alpine performers as well as nordic champions.[14]

In assessing the influence of the Scandinavians, one has to look at the widespread publicity that came in the wake of the various ski carnivals. While attendance figures tend to be unreliable, they do, nonetheless, give a part of the picture. There seems to be little question that thousands of westerners caught the excitement of this new winter sport through watching the likes of a Kaldahl, Ulland, or the "Portland Express" — Hjalmar Hvam. On the jumping hills of Leavenworth, Revelstoke, Hollyburn, or Spokane, their feats were applauded and given colourful commentary in the local press. For example, when Mobraaten captured the Pacific Northwest title in 1934 before an announced crowd of 5,000, the event provoked an effusive tribute: "Mobraaten's performance at Leavenworth is nothing short of remarkable and stamps him as one of the nation's premier ski-riders — probably the best competitive jumper, cross-country and combined man of them all. And he's a little fellow, too, but a human dynamo on the cross-country course and a winged bundle of energy, grace and skill who sweeps competition aside and leaves spectators wildly enthusiastic in admiration of his complete mastery of himself and his skis."[15]

When his colleague, Kaldahl, put on a winning performance in another meet, it was much the same story: "His form was nearly perfect on each of his two jumps. This compact Canadian never wavered. Take-off style was perfection. His push from the nose was high, inspiring. His air technique revealed perfect mastery — even on his short jump, the form was so immaculate the judges gasped admiringly."[16] An historian once suggested, in all seriousness, that the single word "dolichocephalic" accounted for the superiority of Scandinavians as ski jumpers, noting that their dolichocephalic heads "streamlined front to back, split the air like the beaks of eagles."[17]

Fanciful explanations nothwithstanding, ski jumping continued to attract large crowds, including an estimated 22,000 at one ski meet near Spokane.[18] Indeed, the Kongsberg jumpers became such drawing cards that even off-season events headlined their participation. These included jumping at the Golden Gate Exposition on Treasure Island in 1939, which prompted a congratulatory letter to Sotvedt from the provincial mines minister.[19] In June, 1951, Kaldahl and Mobraaten starred at the annual Portland Rose Festival: 23,000 watched in amazement as the skiers soared almost fifty meters on crushed ice from a trestle *inside* the Multnomah Stadium.[20] And, well before the advent of current "hot dog" skiing, Olav Ulland performed flips during a tournament in 1939 in Seattle's Civic Ice Arena.[21] Incidentally, the Ruud brothers routinely did somersaults on the storied Hannibal hill in Kongsberg when they bounced to stop along the outrun![22] Even today, the Kongsberg spirit lives on: at the age of 84 Hvam was recently featured for a television promotion for skiing on Oregon's Mt. Hood. Curious reporters wanted to know if he was a new version of the original who once captured a dozen

consecutive downhill titles in the Pacific Northwest.[23] Then there is Gus
Johnson — name changed from Gudmund Heia for obvious reasons — who
is still directing at the Lac Le Jeune resort where he also ran in the over-80
class of the 1987 marathon![24]

Although the Kongsberg skiers thrived in the ski carnival atmosphere,
they still saw competitive skiing as essentially a week-end activity, as
did most Scandinavians. But the tournaments gave the skiers identity:
Mobraaten, for example, said that he was never out of work once he began
competing. Ulland parlayed his fame as champion into one of the largest
sporting goods enterprises in the northwest — Osborn & Ulland. Hjalmar
Hvam had similar success in Portland following his invention of the first
commercially available safety-ski binding. And Henry Sotvedt teamed up
with Gus Johnson to launch the Two Skiers enterprise in Vancouver after
his years on the ski circuit in Wells and elsewhere. In their capacities as ski
salesmen, these individuals helped to initiate thousands of newcomers into
the mysteries of equipment and technique, both off and on the hills.[25]

One further point is worth noting concerning the Kongsberg contingent,
namely, their work on behalf of organized skiing. A partial listing of
Sotvedt's accomplishments indicates just how far-ranging these activities
could be: western vice-president of the Canadian Amateur Ski Association;
technical chairman and official jumping instructor for the C.A.S.A.; initi-
ator of the junior jumping programme in the high schools; first Canadian
(with Rolf Dokka) to be certified as an international judge by the F.I.S.; first
Canadian to judge in a European championship; coach and manager of the
Canadian team for the 1964 Olympics; delegate to F.I.S. congresses; and
judge for the first ski-flying meet held in North America. In all of activities,
Sotvedt was a tireless ambassador for the sport.

For Henry Sotvedt it had been an eventful odyssey since his departure
from Kongsberg in 1929. He came to Wells in 1935 to work for Caribou Gold
Quartz, and there he met up with the Brandvold brothers, Hegseth, and
Nordal Kaldahl.[26] It was a time, he recalled, when "...we spent the next three
years working in the mines, building ski hills, including a ski cabin in the
summer, and skiing and competing in the winter." As he was to write in later
years, "Almost everyone enjoyed watching a well-executed jump, but no
one could possibly enjoy it as much as the jumper himself." Over the next
two decades Sotvedt amassed dozens of trophies throughout the Pacific
region; as late as the 1950's he was still very much in contention in both
nordic and alpine events, still in the sport for the sheer enjoyment. By the
late 1960's, however, ski jumping had begun to decline. It is ironic that
as Sotvedt gained international recognition for his contributions, the
Kongsberg connection was unable to sustain the nordic thrust in skiing.
Among the last of the jumping meets in the Vancouver area, the Sons of
Norway tournament of January, 1969, was somehow symbolic of the
decline. Sotvedt's good colleague, Kaldahl, had passed away, and he had
often joked that he wanted to have his ashes make that last flight off the

Skiers in Smithers, B.C. 1935. Left to right: R. Stanyer, John Holst, uniden-
tified, Chris Elvenes, Steen Olafson, Chris Dahlie, Knute Nyseen, Per
Sandnes, unidentified.

Ladies cross-country racers, Smithers, B.C. 1935. Left to right: Peggy
Saunders, Peggy Harlin, Beryl McMillan, June McMillan, Alma Pearson.

Henry Sotvedt, Mount Seymour, 1934.

Art Johnson at Nels Nelsen Hill, Revelstoke, B.C. 1940's.

Mt. Seymour take-off, a request that Sotvedt and his fellow skiers honoured as the meet opened.[27]

The traditional practices and attitudes brought in by the Scandinavian immigrants undoubtedly sparked the discovery of skiing as sport in the Pacific Northwest, but tradition itself eventually became a casualty. To explain the virtual disappearance of nordic competition in Washington by the 1970's, Olav Ulland pointed to the persistence of old customs: "The Seattle Ski Club ran cross country races on Saturday, and then jumped on Sunday...They used exactly the same pattern as in Norway."[28] There was no second influx of Old Country skiers prepared to continue the traditional ways. In fact, entrepreneurs such as Franz Wilhelmsen who initiated the Whistler development, and Ornulf Johnsen, known locally as the "Guru of Grouse Mountain," represented the new wave which capitalized on the explosive growth of alpine skiing.[29]

In September, 1973, an event took place which, in retrospect, had a parallel to the decline of nordic skiing. It marked the end of one uniquely Scandinavian venture that epitomized skiing for identity and tradition. The provincial government had just announced the closing down of the Diamond Head chalet. The cost accountants had duly examined the Brandvold brothers' thirty year mountain wilderness experiment and delivered their verdict: "We wonder, in terms of public monies for facilities such as this, just what the priority is...Look at the number of people you're serving — not very many...but I'm sure there will be objections to closing down Diamond Head."[30] For Sotvedt's fellow mine workers — Ottar and Emil Brandvold — it was a poignant final chapter in an immigrant saga which had its origin in the Gudbransdal region of east-central Norway. Ottar responded to the government action, noting, "We did it the hard way. It's a shame all the hard work has to go to waste now. We feel we did a pretty fair job in opening up the area. It made it possible for thousands of people to visit the place — and they all seemed to enjoy themselves."[31]

The Brandvolds emigrated in 1929, going directly to the almost wholly Norwegian town of Frontier, Saskatchewan. Here they worked on a farm, but found out in Ottar's words that "...the worst people you could work for were your own..."[32] Moving westward, they were drawn by stories of gold to Quesnel and the Cottonwood River area of B. C. For the next few years, they worked in the mines of Barkerville and Wells, with plentiful opportunities for skiing in that heavy snow belt region. Both of the Brandvolds ran cross country and jumped; it was a visit to a Banff meet which finally convinced them to search out a location where the best in a skiing tradition — as they saw it — could be sustained in an unspoiled environment. Diamond Head chalet in the Garibaldi alpine meadows was the result. How that came about is also a story of transplanting an approach to skiing as a way of life — an approach not dissimilar to that of the Kongsberg immigrants, despite the absence of the competitive dimension in the Diamond Head enterprise.

The Alpine Club of Canada honoured the Brandvolds in 1972 for their work on behalf of skiing and mountaineering. A club member recalled how "...they built the chalet with hand cut logs, trailed and surveyed the area, and hand-built a seven mile trail to the chalet."[33] That slim description obviously omitted most of the details of an extraordinarily difficult undertaking. The Brandvolds discovered Garibaldi in 1940, then spent the following three winters skiing the region, sizing up its possibilities. The appeal to them must be seen, in part, from the perspective of the Old Country. In Scandinavia, but especially in Norway, the mountain *hytte*, or hut, takes on almost mythic significance — a place for contemplation, and for a special relationship with nature. Ottar has described the idyllic beauty of Garibaldi in the summer, but he has also spoken with exhuberance of their elemental battle with the winter snows: "It snowed almost every day from early November to mid-December. We had to uncover the logs every day, then we had a break...but still had to use lanterns and work all night New Year's Eve (1944) just to get the roof done before the snow came again."

That first winter the Brandvolds guided in some hundred-odd skiers. As many as a dozen at a time would overnight in their small cabin before the chalet was finished — but at no charge for the room! In the years to come, Diamond Head became a mecca for dedicated outdoor enthusiasts: for the Brandvolds it became their life's work, which Ottar described as one of "....hard work, but a good life which allowed us to ski and show people how to enjoy the out of doors." They had the satisfaction of passing on a part of their cultural heritage, and in so doing, established their own identity. The Brandvolds had become a cultural institution.[34]

Much more remains to be said about the role of Scandinavians in the ski history of the west. A more complete story would have many remarkable chapters: they would tell of such characters as *bon vivant*, Per Sandnes, King's Cup winner from Trondheim, equally renowned for his jumping and partying skills; of Nilo Itkonen, Finnish-born Canadian champion of 1952, still competing in the Caribou Marathon; of Galiano resident Earl Young (Odegaard) one time Banff instructor and ski cabin builder on Hollyburn; of Oslo natives Hermod and Magnus Bakke, synonymous with Leavenworth ski history; of Kongsberg sharpshooter and timber cruiser, Harold Orm, who started a ski factory in Smithers; and of Swedish-born, Rudolph Verne, who first saw the winter sports potential above Burrard Inlet. Perhaps with a revived interest in such old fashioned Scandinavian practices as telemark skiing and other joys of skiing in the traditional way, people may be sufficiently curious to ask that these stories be told.[35]

NOTES

1. *Hiker & Skier* April 3, 1936, pp. 11-12.
2. Bruce Kidd, "The Workers' Sport Movement in Canada, 1924-1940: The Radical Immigrants' Alternative," paper presented to the Canadian Ethnic Studies Association, Edmonton, October 14, 1981, p. 1.
3. See special edition *Laagendalsposten,* May 13, 1987, for both historical details on Kongsberg and specific accounts of Kongsberg skiers from 1928 to 1948.
4. Leif Halsnes, "Olaus Jeldness: Champion af Canada i Skilöbning og Hopping," in *Norröna,* February 15, 1979, p. 6. See also Sam Wormington, *The Ski Race* (Sandpoint, Idaho: Selkirk Press Inc., 1980), pp. 7-29.
5. Wormington, pp. 18-19.
6. *Ibid.*
7. *Ibid.,* p. 45.
8. For biographical details on Noren, see Wormington, pp. 50-51. Noren spent some 45 years in Alaska, returned to Norway in 1954, but at his death in 1979, aged 89, was back in the U. S.
9. Wormington, p. 49.
10. Nels Nelsen was inducted into the B. C. Sports Hall of Fame in 1984. In 1925, he set an unofficial world record jump of 240 feet on the Revelstoke hill; he won Canadian titles from 1916 through 1920. See the Nelsen files, B. C. Sports Hall of Fame archives for details.
11. See "Da gamle-gutta möttes," *Laagendalsposten,* June 14, 1985, p. 6; "Canadisk gull til skimuseet," *Laagendalsposten,* June 30, 1986, p. 7; "Ulland donates ski trophies to hometown museum," *Western Viking,* June 19, 1987, p. 3, for details of Kongsberg skiers at home and abroad who participated in the opening of the ski museum. Among those skiers from the Pacific Northwest whose trophies are displayed are Sotvedt, Kaldahl, Mobraaten, Ulland, and Hvam. Interview with Hvam, March 1, 1986.
12. Information on Sotvedt's career is found primarily in the late skier's personal papers made available to me by Mrs. Anne Sotvedt. See also *Nordmanns-Forbundet* (1963) for interview with Sotvedt; *Seattle Post-Intelligencer,* February 11, 1935; *Vancouver News-Herald,* February 24, 1941; and "Idretten hjalp utvandrere gjennom vanskelig °ar," in *Drammens Tidende og Buskeruds Blad* (1975) for additional details.
13. Norman Berger, "the Evolution of a Ski Jumper," *Canadian Ski Annual* (1933), p. 38.
14. Interview with Petter Hugsted, June 23, 1986. On this occasion, Hugsted, 1948 Olympic gold medal winner in jumping, took me to the famed Hannibal Hill in Kongsberg. He explained that in his day, and in the Ruud brothers' era, all jumpers skied to and from the jump hill, becoming adept at downhill and cross-country skiing, as well as jumping.
15. *Leavenworth Echo,* February 16, 1934.
16. *Seattle Times,* February 3, 1933. See also *Vancouver Sun,* March 12, 1934.
17. Joseph T. Hazard, "Winter Sports in the Western Mountains: The Story of the Ski in the Pacific Northwest," *Pacific Northwest Quarterly,* vol. 44, no. 1, (January, 1953), p. 8.
18. Wormington, p. 400.
19. Sotvedt Papers. See ff. 12.
20. Kaldahl Papers, B. C. Sports Hall of Fame archives.
21. Ulland was one of seven ski jumping brothers, all of world class calibre. Ulland achieved instant recognition by being the first jumper to break the 100-meter barrier during a meet in Ponte di Legno, Italy, in 1935. Interview with Olav Ulland, March 1, 1986.
22. *Laagendalsposten,* May 13, 1987.
23. *Western Viking,* December 5, 1986.
24. *The Leiflette District Seven Sons of Norway,* April, 1987.
25. Interview with Ulland, March 1, 1986.
26. Sotvedt Papers. See ff. 12.
27. *Laagendalsposten,* December, 1968.

28. *Normand ved Kysten: The Norwegian Experience in and Around Puget Sound* (Supplement to *Western Viking*), October 10, 1975.

29. See *Vancouver Sun*, December 21, 1985, and Kerry Banks, "The Guru of Grouse" in *Sport'N Style* (Sept. / Oct. 1987), pp. 8-9 for background on Johnsen, and "Dream Built on Snow," *North Shore News*, December 28, 1983, for information on Wilhelmsen.

30. *Vancouver Sun*, September 8, 1973.

31. *Ibid.*

32. Interview with Ottar Brandvold, September 30, 1974. See also *Vancouver Sun*, March 25, 1972, and Sotvedt letter to *Norröna*, May 15, 1976.

33. *Vancouver Sun*, March 25, 1972.

34. Brandvold interview.

35. For example, see *Canadian Ski Annual* (1926 / 27) for reports by and on Verne, *Western Viking*, April 14, 1986, on Magnus and Hermod Bakke, *Hiker & Skier*, December 31, 1937, on Young, and Norrona, November 24, 1932, on Sandnes.

THE DEVELOPMENT OF CURLING IN WESTERN CANADA

Gerald Redmond

In the *Canadian Magazine* of March, 1971, Paul Grescoe commented that: "Any game played by three-quarters of a million people can't be all dull. More Canadians curl than play golf — or any other sport, for that matter — so there must be more to curling than sliding a rock down a sheet of ice."[1] Three years later, this time in *Maclean's* magazine, Jack Ludwig wrote that: "Curling claims to have 800,000 participants — that's one in every 27 Canadians. Its popularity is still growing but even now it probably comes closest to being our true national sport."[2]

By the 1980's more than a million Canadians were regular curlers, an impressive statistic. Whatever "a true national sport" may be, and whatever criteria may be used for determining it (and here most people would probably give ice hockey the nod in Canada, particularly if spectatorship were included in the evaluation) there is no doubt that curling is one of Canada's most popular sports. The evidence would also suggest that a majority of its most significant developments have occurred in Western Canada; and that the Scots deserve the most credit for its origin, diffusion and early success.

Although there is evidence of similar ice games in some European countries from at least the sixteenth-century, authorities are agreed that the sport of curling as we know it was codified in Scotland and from there exported to other countries. In Canada especially curling thrived to an extent unparalleled elsewhere, due to a number of factors, among which were the powerful and ubiquitous Scottish presence, the climate and geography, the democratic nature of the sport itself as well as its traditions, technological advances, and the active patronage of influential persons.[3]

A word or two about the Scots first. While most people might imagine that Scotland's greatest export was Scotch whisky, Professor Gordon Donaldson has shown that it really was *people*. Emigration has been an enduring aspect of Scottish history, and Scots have settled in various parts of the world for a variety of economic, political, religious and social reasons.[4] It has been suggested that wherever they settled — in Australia, Canada, New Zealand or South Africa — they immediately built three structures: a church, for they were a devout people; a school or university, for they had a great respect for education; and a distillery, for they liked to adhere to their native culture... In addition, they naturally fostered their traditional sports, and so the Caledonian, or Highland, Games, curling and golf took root in their new environment.

Almost inevitably, as histories of these countries show, many Scots prospered in the New World. One historian suggests an old Scottish prayer as a partial answer to their success in rugged environments: "O Lord, we do no ask you to give us wealth, only to show us where it is..."[5] Pierre Berton has dwelt at length on the work ethic that to him explains "the dominance of the Scot in pioneer Canada," and stated:

> ...The Irish outnumbered them, as they did the English, but the Scots ran the country. Though they formed only one-fifteenth of the population they controlled the fur trade, the great banking and financial houses, the major educational institutions and, to a considerable degree, the government. The CPR was built to a large extent by Irish navvies and Irish contractors; but it was the Scots who held the top jobs. Almost every member of the original CPR Syndicate was a self-made Scot.[6]

From this establishment position, then, it can be appreciated that Scots in Canada were comfortably situated to indulge their culture, which included their traditional sports.

Reference has already been made to golf, which historians have described as "Scotland's gift to the world" — while curling has been called "Scotland's ain game." Not surprisingly both sports were pioneered in Canada by Scots, but exact origins remain a mystery.

Some historians have suggested, without providing any documentation, that both originated here among Scottish soldiers during the Seven Years' War of 1756-63. This is possible since curling and golf were underway in Scotland before that time, but unlikely in view of the fact that Highlanders were not really involved in either sport. And the enthusiastic suggestion by curling's most comprehensive historian, the Reverend John Kerr, that eighteenth-century Scots were actually *eager* to enlist for active service in British North America because of the curling opportunities afforded them[7] is too far-fetched to take seriously. Henry Roxborough, a prolific author on the history of Canadian sport, has commented that: "Indeed, it seems that if so many firsts in Canadian sport can be traced back to Wolfe's soldiers, it is difficult to comprehend how they found time to pursue their military duties."[8]

While we are speculating, it is interesting to note that others have looked even further back to the contests and feats of the *coureurs de bois* and the *voyageurs*. Kavanagh, in his *History of Golf in Canada* suggests that the fur traders of the seventeenth-century may have imported golf to Canada:

In days lang syne the distant posts of the Hudson's Bay Company
...were almost all manned by Scotchmen...Many of them undoubtedly brought out with them their golf clubs with which to
enjoy even in a most primitive fashion the exhilarating swing and
the "fair follow through" so dear to the heart of the golfer...What
more likely then that the Scotch factors of "The Governor and
Company of Adventurers of England trading into Hudson Bay"
— nearly four centuries ago were the pioneer golfers of America?
That the strident "Fore" was first heard in the spacious West and
that its echo, centuries old, has travelled Eastward only of recent
years? Supposition is strongly in favor of this contention. Proof
of course there is none![9]

Just to imagine the Orkneymen and Highlanders of the Old Company teeing
up in the vast emptiness of the early Northwest Territories is a thought to
boggle the minds of many, comfort some, and possibly disturb others. The
suggestion is made even more intriguing by Kavanagh's statements elsewhere
that the first municipal golf course in Canada opened in Edmonton, Alberta,
on land originally owned by the Hudson's Bay Company, and that "Western
Canada took the lead in establishing public courses."[10]

It would be pleasant to claim here and produce evidence to the effect that
curling really originated in Western Canada, in similar circumstances, but
it is a case of "proof of course there is none." Rather, the available evidence
still favours the formation of the Montreal Curling Club in 1807, by Scottish fur traders, as the legitimate starting point. Then, as with so many other
aspects of Canadian history, a firm foundation was first established in central
Canada — through the formation of clubs and competition, improvement
in equipment and facilities (including the establishment of indoor rinks), and
influential patronage and publicity — before similar developments occurred
in the West. One of the factors which greatly facilitated the spread of curling
in Ontario and Quebec was the growth of railways there, but the second half
of the nineteenth-century was dominated by the completion of Canada's first
transcontinental line, the Canadian Pacific Railway. As it reshaped the
geography and life of the new nation, so it also affected the future of
Canadian sport, including curling.[11]1

By the time the last spike of the CPR was driven home by Donald A.
Smith, later Lord Strathcona, at Craigellachie, in 1885, the railway had
permanently shaped the map of Canada as it was eventually created, and
developed new communities across the three prairie provinces and British
Columbia. The eventual route stretched from Winnipeg through Portage la
Prairie, Brandon, Regina, Moose Jaw, Swift Current, Medicine Hat,
Calgary, Banff, Kamloops, and later to Port Moody and Vancouver.

The acquisitive, energetic and enterprising Scots were active in these new
communities as they had been elsewhere in the Dominion. As well as their
dominant influence in the CPR itself, one Scottish writer, George Bryce, has
been moved to claim: "Perhaps the crowning success of Scottish nationality

in Western Canada is the spread of the great Scottish game of curling." The fact that Bryce was a former skip of the Winnipeg Granite Curling Club gave him "peculiar pleasure in recording the remarkable influence exercised by the game of curling in the west." Despite the probable bias, it was not altogether an exaggeration, and the facts bear out his further contention that:

> Almost every railway town in Western Canada early in its history erects a commodious building, which is flooded on the interior ground floor and forms an ice sheet which lasts, with some addition, for three or four months.[12]

In 1871, a St. Andrew's Society was organized in Winnipeg, and Donald A. Smith was its first president. The start of curling was organized in Manitoba a few years later, and Smith became a patron, using some of the wealth gained from his railway enterprises to donate the Strathcona Cup and sponsor the sport in other ways as well. Writing in *Outing* magazine in 1895, Henry Woodside observed that Sir Donald A. Smith, K.C.M.G., was:

> among the most eminent patrons and curlers of the Northwest...His home is now in Montreal, but he has a warm feeling for the Province in which the most of his busy life was spent. He is an ardent friend of the Bonspiel and of the game.

Woodside also claimed: "Curling has been more or less in vogue in the Red River settlement since the early part of the century, and has been regularly played in Winnipeg since before the eighties."[13] However, it was not until 11 December 1876, that "the first official game" was played at the Manitoba Curling Club rink in Winnipeg. Subscriptions from the seventy members had made the erection of the rink possible, and before the year ended "arrangements had been made to curl by artificial light." The game lasted two hours and the losers donated their prize, a barrel of oatmeal, to the hospital.[14]

Such charity was not unusual in Scottish sports, but it must be recorded that a more common feature was a generous prize list in their competitions. Monetary prizes, and items of considerable value, were often objects of such Scottish sporting endeavor in Canada, as they were in Scotland itself. Certainly many true enthusiasts also participated without any form of profitable inducements, but prizes were a noticeable feature in most cases.

By 1889, for example, sixty-two rinks gathered at the Winnipeg Bonspiel for three days of competition "for magnificent trophies and numerous gold and silver medals."[15] Largely because of its generous prizes the Winnipeg Bonspiel "was the curlers' delight." In 1901 some of the "loot" included:

First Prize: Challenge Cup, value $250.00 and four diamond pins, value $100.00 each.
Second Prize: Four pearl-handled umbrellas — $50.00 each.
Third Prize: Four brass kettles — $50.00 each.
Fourth Prize: Four Bronze statuettes — $30.00 each.

The Innisfail, Alberta, Curling Club rink, winners of The Calgary Brewing and Malting Company's Cup at the Wetaskiwin Bonspiel in 1904. Left to right: W.J. Curry, H.M. Douglas, C.B. McCallum and F.J. Dobson. Credit: Glenbow-Alberta Institute Archives

There were many other valuable prizes, and each prize bore a value tag.[16]

The development toward such opulence was quite spectacular. In fact, the charter members of the Manitoba Curling Club initiated perhaps the most prodigious and successful growth of any single sport, associated with a particular area, anywhere in the world. In the latter part of the nineteenth-century the CPR established Winnipeg; in the early twentieth-century the province of Manitoba was the established world centre for the sport of curling. This dominant position was determined even before the Scottish curling influence in Canada was climaxed by the first tour of a Scottish team in 1902-3.

February 13, 1884, "was a red-letter day in the curling history of Manitoba when a grand Provincial Bonspiel was opened." The play lasted two days and ended with a "sumptuous banquet" enjoyed by the members of clubs from Brandon, Emerson, Portage la Prairie, Stonewall, Stony Mountain, and Winnipeg. Other curling clubs were also formed within the next few years.[17]

Their success in an international bonspiel at St. Paul led directly to the formation of the Manitoba Branch of the Royal Caledonian Curling Club, instituted on 6 December 1888, at a meeting in the rooms of the Winnipeg Granite Club. This branch was noted as "having for its territory a district larger than many a world-famous kingdom — from Port Arthur to Calgary, nearly fifteen hundred miles."[18] In years to come, the area was to become equally distinguished by its number of participants. In fact, by 1896, the Winnipeg Granites were numerically the strongest curling club in all Canada. Four years earlier, Hedley had observed:

> People in Ontario consider that province in an especial degree the home of curling. Many of them will be surprised, however, on learning what strides the game has taken in the far West, and how active and enterprising its votaries are. There are fifteen clubs in Manitoba and eight in the territories of Assiniboia and Alberta, the active membership of which twenty-three clubs is over 1,200.[19]

Ontario had about a hundred clubs in the 1890's against approximately half that number in the rest of Canada. Toronto had six curling clubs, "all in excellent working order," by 1884, and was the headquarters of curling in Ontario. One of the original members of the Toronto Granite Club, formed in 1875, was no less than John A. Macdonald, Canada's first Prime Minister, and other eminent public figures also belonged.[20] But by the turn of the century the spotlight was moving inexorably towards Winnipeg. The historian Kerr, captain of the visiting Scottish team to Canada in 1902-3, was much impressed by the palatial premises owned by the Toronto curling clubs, but Kerr observed that "it seemed to him that the interest in curling increased the farther they went west."

When the team did proceed "far West to Winnipeg" his tendency to use superlatives in praise of Scottish Canadian curling knew no bounds.

"Undoubtedly," said Kerr, "Winnipeg is the very fireplace or hearth of the game in the Dominion." Significantly, he went much further: "Winnipeg was indeed the mecca of curlers all over the world," where curling was "conducted on a scale unequalled anywhere else in the world," and the place where "one meets the finest curlers and sees the finest curling in the world." Finally, and this was another large and generous admission for an ambassador of the mother club in Scotland to make, "Winnipeg was the summit and acme and climax of all."[21] If this were not true then, it was certainly confirmed later. By 1950, Winnipeg had more curling clubs than Montreal and Toronto combined, and there were more in Manitoba than in the whole of Ontario and Quebec. In the 1949-50 season, the Flin Flon Curling Club claimed to be "the largest individual curling club in the world, with 121 regular men's and 40 ladies' rinks." The bonspiel entry for the Manitoba Curling Association in 1948, its Diamond Jubilee Year, was, in fact, a world record.[22]

Before it became "the very fireplace or hearth of the game in the Dominion" in 1903, Winnipeg was the springboard from which curling moved further west, via the rails of the Canadian Pacific Railway. Under the heading of "Curliana," a reporter in the Calgary *Herald* of 30 November 1883 asked: "Would it not be well for those of our citizens who participate in the 'roarin' game' to meet together and discuss the propriety of forming a curling Club?" This was formed in 1885, and plans were made to form a joint stock company which would sell shares to finance the erection of an enclosed rink. The stock company was registered as the Alberta Rink Company, and the new rink was completed in 1890. In the meantime the curling club had used the Star Skating Rink, and competed in the Winnipeg bonspiel.[23]

In 1884, the Edmonton *Bulletin* reported a curling match in Prince Albert East, in which "Canada scored 29 against Scotland 16," indicating a Scottish presence there.[24] A group of Scots was definitely the founders of the Edmonton Curling Club. The Edmonton *Bulletin* of December 1, 1888, announced there would be a public meeting "for the purpose of organizing a skating and curling club...to be held in McDonald's and McLeod's office tonight." The same issue carried a report of what was described as "the first curling match in Northern Alberta" by a group of Scots celebrating St. Andrew's Day, when there were a large number of spectators present, many of them ladies. Whatever may have happened in McDonald's and McLeod's office, it was the gentlemen of the St. Andrew's Society of Edmonton who formed a club, and a year later the monthly meeting of the Edmonton Curling Club was held November 8, 1889, when the contractors had completed construction of the curling rink said to be "the best of its kind in the Territories."[25]

Seventy-two years later, the Edmonton *Journal* of March 10, 1961, carried the reminiscences of a 92-year-old original club member (Arthur Omsley) who described curlers using kettles filled with sand. Later, blacksmiths were persuaded to provide stones made from iron blocks with handles welded on

*Group of men curlers outside curling rink in Calgary, c. 1890's. (Colonel
James Walker is in the centre row, fourth from the left.)
Credit: Glenbow-Alberta Institute Archives*

to them. Moccasins, household brooms and oil lanterns were also common-
place for these outdoor pioneers curling on the North Saskatchewan River.

Other curlers were on the river at Medicine Hat in 1889, although a club
was not formed until 1896. Also in 1896, curling took place in Banff, where
a club was formed before 1900. A Lethbridge Curling Club was organized
in 1889, and eight years later opened an indoor rink, complete with electric
light. The Fort Macleod Club also opened a rink in 1898, and a curling club
was formed in Anthracite the following year. The Calgary bonspiel of that
year had rinks competing from Edmonton, Fort Macleod, Fish Creek,
Lethbridge, Innisfail, and Golden, British Columbia.

The Golden Curling Club was formed during the winter of 1895-96, along
with others at Nelson and Sandon. These were preceded only by a club
consisting of sixteen members at Kaslo, who obtained their rocks from
Winnipeg.[26] Elsewhere in British Columbia: "The first curling in Armstrong,
January, 1897, was held in a cattle barn built by Wood Argill Co. The rocks
were turned by Mr. Norman McLeod from a birch log and handles put in
by the blacksmith."[27] The Kootenay Curling Association was organized at
a meeting in the Allan Hotel at Rossland, on 12 February 1898, which took
place during "the first bonspiel to be held in British Columbia," when
eighteen rinks representing four communities took part. Ten years later, this
association became the British Columbia Curling Association and affiliated
with the Royal Caledonian Curling Club.[28]

By March 1891, the editor of *The Dominion Illustrated* claimed that "curling has spread through the land from Dan to Beersheba," and certainly by the end of the century, indoor curling was established as a Dominion-wide sport.

A eulogy of sport in British Columbia, written by a gentleman in 1898, mentioned "the roaring game played by the inferior sex" in that province.[29] It was indicative of an attitude toward women at a time when usually "men performed on the tourney fields of sport under the approving and admiring gaze of ladies." But in the second half of the nineteenth century a favourable change in the attitude of society toward women's participation in sport became apparent, and one of the sports in which women gained their athletic emancipation was curling.

It has been suggested that the consumption of "copious quantities of whisky during the matches" was the main reason that curling was initially a game for men only, and that ladies only became enthusiastic spectators as this habit began to wane.[30] In 1890, a Montreal club sponsored a gala ladies' night to which it invited one hundred guests and "dainty hands clapped warmly to encourage the players."[31] But by this time many dainty hands had also steered bicycles, thrown balls, held hockey sticks and wielded golf clubs, so it was not long before the ladies also participated in curling. There were women curlers and clubs in several parts of western Canada by 1900, and Kerr and his Scottish party enjoyed the hospitality and competition provided by female curlers during their tour of Canada in 1902-3. Several photographs of ladies' curling clubs are included in his book of the tour. And a women's rink from Quebec *defeated* the visitors, causing them to point out that the women had used small iron stones about half the size and weight of those used by the Scotsmen!

In this century, it is no exaggeration to maintain that western Canada has featured — even dominated — in practically all of the sport's major developments. A Dominion Championship competition was inaugurated in 1927, sponsored by the W. D. Macdonald (Tobacco) Company for a trophy known as the Macdonald Brier Tankard. This annual event — now referred to simply as "the Brier" — gave curling a significant impetus, and includes one representative rink from each province, plus an extra one from Northern Ontario. In 1975, a rink was entered from the Northwest Territories and Yukon, also, making a total of 12 teams. The winner of the Brier represents Canada in the World Curling Championship — which was known as the Scotch cup from 1959-1968, then the Silver Broom. During the 1940s, outdoor curling with cement-filled jam tins became a craze across the Prairies, and in 1947 the first "Carspiel" was held at Nipawin, Saskatchewan, with four Hudson sedans valued at $2200 each as prizes. In 1969, the Ken Watson rink from Manitoba was the first to win the Brier three times. The Matt Baldwin rink from Alberta also won 3 times in 1954, 1957 and 1958 — and Ernie Richardson's rink from Saskatchewan won four Briers in the five years between 1959 and 1963. Later, the Ron Northcott rink from Alberta was

Women curling at Banff, Alberta in 1903. The rink was located on a slough near the boat house. Note the lighting arrangements.
Credit: Glenbow-Alberta Institute Archives

Interior of the Edmonton curling rink, showing women curling, March 1929.
Credit: Glenbow-Alberta Institute Archives. (McDermid Collection)

another three times winner. In short, western provinces have dominated the Brier. From its inception in 1927 to 1986, the leaders have been Manitoba with 22 wins, Alberta with 14, and Saskatchewan with 7. And, although competition has been tougher in recent years, Canadian teams, represented mostly by Western rinks, have also dominated World Championship competition since its beginning in 1959.

By any criteria, Canada is now the major home of this sport and the Scottish bagpipes, heard at any one of hundreds of bonspiels across the country, is the most obvious symbolic reminder of its heritage.[32]

In conclusion, it is more than appropriate that *curling* should have been chosen as the demonstration sport for winter Olympic Games in 1988, and that those games should have been held in a western Canadian city. Canadians from Manitoba may have felt envious, of course, given the unequalled contribution of that province in the history of curling. Yet the Calgary Olympic bonspiel of 1988 is undoubtedly destined to become another landmark in the development of curling in Western Canada. Thus the Canadian dominance of the sport internationally has been molded nationally by the regional dominance of western Canadians, both as competitors and as innovators in this colourful winter sport.

NOTES

1. Paul Grescoe, "Any Game Played by 750,000 People Can't Be All Dull," *Canadian Mazagine*, 6 March 1971, pp. 7-9.
2. Jack Ludwig, "Rocks of All Ages." *Maclean's*, February 1974, pp. 26-29.
3. See in Gerald Redmond, *The Sporting Scots of Nineteenth-Century Canada*. (Chapter 3, entitled "Curling,") (London and Toronto: Associated University Presses, 1982), pp. 104-158.
4. Gordon Donaldson, *The Scots Overseas*. (London: Robert Hale, 1966).
5. As quoted in John Murray Gibbon, *Canadian Mosaic: The Makings of a Northern Nation*. (Toronto: McClelland and Stewart, 1964), p. 78.
6. Pierre Berton, *The National Dream: The Great Railway, 1871-1881*. (Toronto: Ryerson Press, 1966), p. 319.
7. John Kerr, *History of Curling*. (Edinburgh: David Douglas, 1890), p. 323.
8. Henry Roxborough, *One Hundred Not Out: The Story of Nineteenth-Century Canadian Sport*. (Toronto: Ryerson Press, 1966), p. 105.
9. L. V. Kavanagh, *History of Golf in Canada*. (Toronto: Fitzhenry and Whiteside, 1973), pp. x-xi.
10. *Ibid*, pp. 147-148.
11. Redmond, pp. 108-137.
12. George Bryce, *The Scotsman in Canada*, Vol. 2. (Toronto: Musson Book Company, 1911), pp. 417-418.

13. Henry J. Woodside, "Curling in the Northwest, Part 1," *Outing*, February, 1895, p. 422.
14. W. A. Creelman, *Curling, Past and Present*. (Toronto: McClelland and Stewart, 1950), pp. 142-143.
15. Woodside, p. 423.
16. Roxborough, p. 103.
17. Creelman, p. 143.
18. Woodside, p. 423.
19. J. Hedley, "Curling in Canada, Part II." *Dominion Illustrated Monthly 1*, 1892, pp. 173-182.
20. John A. Stevenson, *Curling in Ontario, 1846-1946.* Toronto: Ontario Curling Association, *passim.*
21. Kerr, *passim.*
22. Creelman, pp. 144-145.
23. Calgary *Herald*, 9 January, 1889; and 6 March, 1889.
24. Edmonton *Bulletin*, 9 February, 1884.
25. Edmonton *Bulletin*, 9 November, 1889.
26. Redmond, p. 136.
27. Johnny Serra, *The History of Armstrong, British Columbia.* Okanagan Historical Society, n.d., p. 18.
28. Creelman, p. 151.
29. Thomas L. Grahame, "National Sport: Pastimes in British Columbia." *Canadian Magazine*, March 1989, p. 464.
30. Margaret Ann Hall, "A History of Women's Sport in Canada Prior to World War I." Unpublished M.A. Thesis, University of Alberta, 1968, p.101.
31. Montreal Gazette, 21 February, 1890.
32. Gerald Redmond, "Curling," in *The Canadian Encyclopedia*, Second Edition, Vol. 1. Edmonton: Hurtig Publishers, 1988, pp. 555-556.

THE DEVELOPMENT OF SPEED SKATING IN WESTERN CANADA FROM A PERSONAL PERSPECTIVE

Doreen Ryan

Doreen Ryan has been a speedskater for twenty-five years, and during that time she won fourteen Canadian championships. She also won one North American championship, was runner-up in another, but was not able to go to the World Championships as there was never enough money. However, she represented Canada in two Olympic Games, in 1960 and 1964, and at both she placed ninth.

She is an all-round athlete, having competed in many sports including fastball and basketball. And she won the Canadian Junior Track and Field Championships in 1947, the same year that she won her first Canadian speedskating junior championship. She is a member of the City of Edmonton Sports Hall of Fame, the Alberta Sports Hall of Fame, and the Canadian Speedskating Hall of Fame.

Ryan was born and raised in Edmonton and has spent most of her life in that city, but she was living in Calgary at the time of the sports history conference as she was the supervisor of the Olympic Village for the Winter Olympics.

Speedskating in western Canada, in its initial form, can be said to date back to Confederation. In order to set the scene, let's take a quick look at the beginning of skating in Canada, then the emergence of skating and speed-skating in the West to the present.

The first record of skates in North America was in 1604. They had a wooden frame, screwed into the heel of a boot, and strapped on with leather fasteners. Later they were made of metal and were somewhat cumbersome, but were a great improvement over the wood. John Forbes of Dartmouth, Nova Scotia, patented his design of these skates in 1860.

Skating was done on frozen ponds, rivers and lakes, and was frequently a means of travel rather than for pleasure. In the mid-1800s it started to develop into a pleasurable pastime. The heavy snows which accumulated on the frozen rivers and lakes spoiled the ice for skating, and eventually led to the development of ice rinks. These were little more than large sheds constructed over sheets of natural ice. Montreal was the site of the first rink which was built in 1859. A few years later the Victoria Rink was built in the same city. The social set held fabulous skating masquerades, dances and fancy-dress affairs in this gas-lit structure. Nova Scotia and New Brunswick soon arrived on the scene, when a private rink was built in Halifax in 1863, and the first circular type of rink made its appearance in Saint John. Montreal's third rink, built in 1864, advertised "Good Band" twice a week.

The first indication of a skating race in Canada was a race from Montreal to Quebec, down the St. Lawrence River, in 1854. In 1883 an organized speedskating competition was held in the Victoria Rink in New Brunswick. They held a marathon the following year in Saint John. It was a ten-hour race, and the winner skated 117 miles. It went by time rather than distance — how far a competitor could go in that ten hour period. The Amateur Skating Association of Canada, formed in 1887, covered both figure skating and speedskating. The first senior and junior championships were held by the association's Race and Tournament Committee the following year.

This was a picture of the national scene when western Canada came into the picture. The first covered rink in western Canada was built in Winnipeg in 1874. This was followed by one in Regina in 1880. They were even popular in B. C. The Hastings Hotel on the Burrard Inlet advertised an attached rink for the pleasure of guests — weather permitting!

After Confederation, winter social life centered around skating parties, balls and carnivals. The more avid and skilled skaters created a variety of games and activities on ice — such as hurdle races over stiff barriers, skating backwards races, and barrel races. Flour barrels, with the ends removed, were placed at strategic places around the rink. The skater would race to the barrel, crawl through it, get up and skate to the next barrel and repeat the procedure. Barrel jumping was a very exciting event for both spectators and competitors; the faster the skating, the more barrels jumped. Skating became a very popular sport, particularly for women, as it was one of the few sports considered to be lady-like.

It was this carnival-like atmosphere that I remember when I skated in my first race. At that time all community leagues had skating rinks and held annual winter carnivals. Racing was a part of the carnival. The winners went on to the annual Federation of Community Leagues Carnival which was held in the comfort of the indoor city arena. This was a two-day affair which included an official opening, a parade of clowns, a fancy-dress competition, a major figure-skating production, speedskating races, barrel jumping, jumping through hoops of flame, and the crowning of the Federation of Community League Queen. It was at this carnival, held in Edmonton in 1939, where I won my first race, a one-lap race for the under-eight-year olds.

The growth of hockey during the last half of the nineteenth century caused distress to recreational skaters as they lost a lot of ice time. Hockey became

Skating on the Elbow River on a Sunday afternoon in Calgary, 1914-15.
Looking south-west, the large house on the right is on Rideau Road.
Credit: Glenbow-Alberta Institute Archives.

Winter carnival at the Glenora skating rink, Edmonton, February 1926.
Credit: Glenbow-Alberta Institute Archives. (McDermid Collection)

a more lucrative attraction, so rink owners provided more time for them and less ice time for recreational skaters. Also, more skaters went into hockey rather than into speedskating.

In the meantime, serious speedskating was occurring in Winnipeg, where the Canadian Indoor Championships were held in 1922. Frank Stack, from Winnipeg, made a name for himself by winning the North American Indoors Championship in 1931, 1932 and 1934. In 1937, he won the North American Outdoors Championship and competed in the 1936, 1948 and 1952 Olympics. He coached the Canadian 1960 Olympic team, of which I was a member.

Speedskating began to develop in Alberta where inter-club and inter-city meets developed out of the carnival atmosphere, and eventually a provincial championship was organized. Calgary and Edmonton, as well as Banff, Canmore and other small towns competed in all these competitions. The first out-of-province team I remember coming to Edmonton was in 1945 when Saskatoon sent a team to compete at the Edmonton Gardens, and the following year I went on my first skating trip to Saskatoon to compete in their large arena. We had always worked out on hockey rinks, but Saskatoon built a "six-lap to the mile rink," a milestone in speedskating in western Canada. This led to the end of eastern domination in the sport. In 1947, the Canadian championships were held in Sudbury, Ontario, the last one held in eastern Canada for a number of years. Manitoba, Alberta and Saskatchewan became the driving force.

Edmonton built a larger track (six laps to the mile) after Don Wynn and I won the Canadian Championships in Sudbury in 1947. There was no club house, however, and it was difficult lacing up our skates with frozen fingers while sitting in a snow bank. The trials for the 1960 Olympics were held on this track in 1959, but by then we had a club house with a heater. This was the first time there were speedskating competitions for women in the Olympics, and it was also the first time that Olympic-style skating was used in a competitive sense in Canada. This is the skating that we see now, two-lane, two people on the track, with the competitors racing against time. Previously there was a "mass start," like a horse race, or a track race but without individual lanes. Competitors drew numbers for their position on the starting line, and as soon as the race started, everyone aimed for the corner. In Canada, a great deal of controversy arose with the advent of Olympic-style skating. Competitions were held in both mass start and Olympic-style until the Canadian Amateur Speedskating Association ruled that Olympic style would be used for over sixteen years of age and mass start for under sixteen. Generally, too, mass starts were used on indoor tracks and Olympic-style outdoors.

The first time I saw a 400-metre speedskating track was at the Olympics in Squaw Valley in 1960, and it was mind boggling. It was a big difference from the six lap track — different in the radius of the corners, in the length of the straight-away, and in the entire configuration. The following year

Doreen Ryan, champion speed skater, Edmonton, 1952.

Doreen Ryan, champion speed skater in action, circa. 1960.

Edmonton city built a 400-metre oval, as did various other centres over the years, and speedskating became an established sport in most western Canadian centres. Calgary always had a hard time because the chinooks "blew out" every track they laid. This remained a problem until the new indoor Olympic Oval was constructed.

National Indoor Championships continued to be held, but were low key for a number of years until 1979 when the first official World Indoor Championships was held in the east. Canada was one of the dominating forces. Winnipeg, Saskatoon and Regina produced top skaters in what is now referred to as short-track speedskating. On the international scene, western countries won seventeen World Cup medals, while eastern block countries won two. This "balance of power" changed in 1984 and the situation is now reversed.

This will be the first Olympic championships held indoors, in this fine, new and efficient Olympic Oval. In 1987, the World Championships were held in an indoor facility in Holland and many records were broken there, as indoor ice is generally faster than outdoors. It will be really exciting to watch the further development of speedskating in this province and in Canada generally as a result of this new building.

Not only have the facilities developed from the small outdoor hockey rinks to the vast expanse of the Calgary Indoor Olympic Oval, but clothing has changed from the heavy and bulky, but warm, outfits to the sleek, one-piece body suit. We wore men's long underwear — you couldn't get women's underwear then — and dyed them black. I wore black velveteen shorts over the top of them, and a heavy sweater. Skates have changed somewhat, but not drastically. Part of the boot is now molded. The whole boot cannot be molded as you need the ankle flexibility in skating. The boot is short, just up to the ankle bone, and it can be laced loosely to increase the flexibility if required.

Financially, the life of a speedskater has changed considerably. We used to pay a fee of ten cents per entry, and fifty cents for an amateur card. Now there is a system of carding athletes, and they are paid their expenses each month in an amount based on their previous year's record. There are now paid coaches and an administrative staff. How things have changed since the 1932 Olympics when the International Skating Union telegraphed back to Canada that Frank Stack couldn't compete until the Canadian Amateur Skating Association paid its dues of fifty dollars. To get to North American championships we sold raffle tickets. I spent three days and nights sitting on a Greyhound bus to get to my first North American championship at Alpena, Michigan, and then had to race the first morning after I arrived. In 1968, at the Grenoble Olympics, each individual club was required to subsidize its own Olympic athletes to the tune of five hundred dollars, a ruling which was particularly hard on the Winnipeg Speedskating Club as it had four competitors that year. Now the International Skating Union receives a great deal of money from television rights. The Canadian Speedskating

Association and the Canadian Olympic Association now receive better financial support as well.

There were many "good things about the old days," but thank goodness we don't have to live them again — although there is something to be said for being a pioneer in a sport. It will be very interesting to follow the progress of speedskating in western Canada with the beautiful facility in Calgary. Technique will improve, records will be broken and training will be considerably easier in a warm atmosphere. However, I do have one concern that our skaters will not be as "tough," particularly if they have to skate outdoors in winter conditions.

THE PROBLEMS OF PROFESSIONALISM:
THE MANITOBA AMATEUR ATHLETIC ASSOCIATION
AND THE FIGHT AGAINST PRO HOCKEY, 1904-1911

Morris Mott

On March 28, 1911, President J. D. Pratt of the Manitoba Amateur Athletic Association presented his organization's fourth annual report to delegates assembled in a room in Winnipeg's Royal Alexandra Hotel. He referred to the "most satisfactory" condition that prevailed "in nearly all branches of sport" in Manitoba. He spoke with particular enthusiasm about the situation in hockey. Amateur hockey had never been healthier, he said. The reason for this state of affairs was that about three years ago, "in spite of strenuous opposition," the Manitoba Amateur Athletic Association had decided "to fight to revive amateur hockey." The professional element so dominated the sport at that time that it was all but impossible "for our young men to compete in an amateur...game." Now, in 1911, professional hockey could hardly be found. Thanks to the MAAA young Manitobans were again playing the national sport "honestly and fairly, purely for the love of the game, and without any thought of a monetary consideration for their services."[1]

J. D. Pratt, like most historians, altered the truth a bit when he interpreted the past, or at least he exaggerated some truths and ignored or camouflaged others. Nevertheless, his description of the recent hockey history of his province was reasonably accurate. Professional hockey had been prevalent in Manitoba from about 1905 to 1909. Then in the next two years it had disappeared, and it had faded away partly because the officers of the MAAA had fought professionalism with determination and even enthusiasm.

This paper is about the MAAA's struggle against professional hockey. It does not outline the chronology of that struggle. Instead, it describes the reasons for the fight against professionalism and gives some idea of who supported the fight and who opposed it. In doing so, I hope the paper provides interesting and useful information on the following four subjects: 1) the attitudes toward sports that prevailed in the West in the early twentieth century; 2) the changes that were taking place in those attitudes; 3) the nature

Victoria Hockey Club, Winnipeg Senior Team. 1906-1907. Left to right. Back row: G.H. Stead (Treasurer), D.H. Bain (Hon. President), W.E. Robinson (Point). K.L. Patton (Left wing). C.C. Robinson (Secretary-Treasurer), H. Sullivan (Trainer). Middle row: L.M. Moffat (Cover Point), G.A. Wickson (Right wing). J.L. Pratt (President), Grover Sargent (Centre), B.S. Baker (Goal). Front row: Charles Belcher (Left wing), C. Borland (Rover, Captain), F. Caldwell (Centre). Credit: Western Canada Pictorial Index.

of early pro hockey; and 4) Manitoban society, especially the rural-urban tensions and animosities that have been such a prominent feature of life in that province.

The Manitoba Amateur Athletic Association was first formed early in 1904. It was active for a few months, then became invisible until early in 1907 — this explains why J. D. Pratt referred to his 1911 annual report as the fourth annual report of the association. In both 1904 and 1907, the MAAA was founded in order to apply in Manitoba the rules of an organization named the Canadian Amateur Athletic Union.[2]

The Canadian Amateur Athletic Union had been founded in 1884. Originally, it had been essentially a central Canadian organization designed to administer track and field. However, over the years the CAAU's definition of an amateur had been used by clubs, leagues, and associations in various sports across the country. By early in the twentieth century, sports organizations commonly affiliated with the CAAU or asked it to rule on the eligibility of athletes whose amateur status had been questioned.[3]

In both 1904 and 1907 the individuals who established the MAAA believed the CAAU needed help. In 1904, devoted amateurs in Manitoba felt that recently the CAAU had not ruled strictly or quickly enough in dealing with Western athletes.[4] Then in 1907, the MAAA was re-created partly to make sure that the CAAU rules on amateurism were applied by men who knew the Western situation, and also because the CAAU needed assistance in its jurisdictional and philosophical dispute with the newly-formed Amateur Athletic Federation of Canada.[5]

The dispute was over the definition of an amateur. The CAAU's definition by this time read as follows:

> An amateur is a person who has not competed in any competition for a staked bet, monies private or public, or gate receipts, or competed with or against a professional for a prize; who has never taught or assisted in the pursuit of any athletic exercise or sport as a means of livelihood; who has never, directly or indirectly, received any bonus as a payment in lieu of loss of time while playing as a member of any club, or any money consideration whatsoever for any services as an athlete except his actual travelling and hotel expenses, or who has never entered into any competition under a name other than his own, or who has never been guilty of selling or pledging his prizes.[6]

The AAFC's definition of an amateur was virtually the same as this one, except it allowed for amateurs and professionals to play with and against each other — essentially, the AAFC's professional was someone who was paid for playing or winning. Devoted amateurs in Manitoba felt it was important that the CAAU and its strict definition prevail over the AAFC and its more lenient one. They got their wish in 1909, when the CAAU and

AAFC amalgamated largely on the CAAU's terms and formed the Amateur Athletic Union of Canada.[7]

The officers and supporters of the MAAA stood for a strict definition of amateurism, and for minimal contact between paid and unpaid players, because they wanted to discourage young men from becoming professionals and wanted to make it difficult for professionals to influence amateurs. They believed that professional sport was an unfortunate phenomenon — if it was not something evil or immoral it was at least undesirable. What was it about professional sport and professional athletes that bothered them?

Some of the devoted amateurs felt that the existence of professional sport and professional athletes revealed misplaced social and personal priorities. They assumed that sports were not to be taken seriously, but rather should be amusements or diversions. As the editor of the *Hartney Star* suggested in 1907, anyone who worked hard to become good at sports was wasting his time and energy, since nobody would benefit from his dedication. There was important work to perform in the world; professional athletes should start doing some of it.[8]

The notion that sports ought to be diversions appears time and again in early twentieth century negative comments on professional sport. However, by this time most supporters of pure amateurism did not regard sports as frivolous activities. They saw sports as weighty, even vital productions. They believed that sports were valuable and effective educational media. Sports dramatized important truths about life, and inculcated certain qualities in men and even in women that would help them succeed in life. In November of 1908, R. O. Joliffe, a teacher at Winnipeg's Wesley College, wrote an article entitled "On Sport" which summed up the sentiments on sports of hundreds of early twentieth-century writers, preachers, and speakers from Manitoba, the Canadian West, and the entire English-speaking world:

> Whatever a teacher may say of the value of consistent, regular and sustained work in matters intellectual, whatever a preacher may say about laying aside every weight and running the race set before us with endurance — all that is more or less discounted by those who hear us; they expect us to say it. Yet, after all, it is a lesson that only experience can teach, experience for whose tutoring we may pay a high price oftimes where the things of the mind and the spirit are involved; and nowhere is it better taught or more easily learned than in the school of sport. The necessity of constant practice, of steady work, of united effort, sometimes of supreme endeavours in a crisis, is so elemental there, that the analogy between pastimes and life in its more serious aspects is drawn directly and with power."[9]

Sports revealed that success went to those who had certain skills or attributes and who applied them. No, it was not wrong to work hard to develop those skills or attributes; in fact the skills or attributes could be developed only through hard work. It was wrong, however, to take money for displaying them. A fine athlete should be satisfied with the respect and admiration he received from his community. While he might appreciate trophies and different kinds of mementos, he should not want money. In sports, perhaps even more than in other human activities, the desire for money was the "root of all evil." The evil usually manifested itself in the form of violence, broken contracts, and fixed matches.

One of the supporters of the MAAA was the famous Winnipeg Presbyterian clergyman, C. W. Gordon. His attitudes toward sports and professional sports were typical of those held by pure amateurs. He was an assiduous promoter of what he called "clean" sports because he believed that when played and organized properly games could "instill the essentials of true manhood."[10] The novels he wrote under the pen-name Ralph Connor were often peopled by heroes whose manly qualities were revealed in and, we are led to believe, instilled by sports. One thinks of "Shock" Macgregor, hero of *The Prospector*, whom we are first led to admire because of his behaviour as anchor of the Varsity rugby team's "scrum" and then, once he becomes a Presbyterian clergyman in the mining camps of the Rockies, because of his dedication and success in "prospecting" for the souls of men. One thinks also of Corporal Cameron of *Corporal Cameron of the North West Mounted Police*, who is introduced as a Scottish lad who gains self-knowledge through rugby and goes on to become a principled, courageous Mountie in the Canadian West.[11] Through his novels as well as through his activities with the Manitoba Curling Association and the Presbyterian Athletic and Literary Association, Gordon delivered the message that sports were praiseworthy because they tested, instilled, revealed the value of, qualities that were necessary in all of life.

But Gordon had no use for professionalism. "I regard professionalism as the curse of athletics and all true sport," he once wrote. "The moment the taint of professionalism appears, men cease to be interested primarily in the game. [Their interest is] directed to the element of profit in the game, and this creates a determination to win a game at all costs and all hazards. The spirit of chivalry, the sense of fair play, regard for honor, and often regard for human life, all these are sacrificed to the winning of the game, and this means that the game exerts an influence at once brutalizing and degrading."[12] Gordon did not add, but other opponents of professionalism certainly did, that a man who would do anything to win would also take money to lose or to fail to appear for a match.

The pure amateurs thus knew why they disapproved of professional sport. The important questions are, then, who were the pure amateurs, and for whom did they speak? The answer to the first question is, the officers of the MAAA from 1904 through 1914 were almost all British-Protestant business and professional men. They and their most vocal supporters were doctors, lawyers, journalists, school teachers, clerks, insurance agents or

Reverend Charles William Gordon (author Ralph Connor) in 1913. Pastor of St. Stephen's Presbyterian Church, Winnipeg. Credit: Western Canada Pictorial Index.

other private businessmen. They were members of the "middle class" or even "upper class." For whom did they speak? In a way, they were advocates for everyone interested in sports, because sports fans then were very conscious of the problems of professionalism. Many of them carried around in their heads an erroneous interpretation of ancient history which attributed the decay of classical Greek civilization to the rise of professional practices in sports.[13] If they had not actually seen fixed professional matches they had no doubt read about them in their newspapers. They knew that professional players might jump from team to team during a single season, a practice caused primarily by the absence of an overall continental structure to professional sports, and one that suggested that the athletes and the owners were motivated only by money. The followers of sports knew also that, in games in which body contact was allowed, professional contests featured more violence than amateur ones, and then as now, violence sometimes escalated to a point that could bother even a bloodthirsty audience. Early professional sport could produce developments that disgusted virtually everyone. To document this, one need only look at what happened during the Manitoba Professional Hockey League's season of 1907-08.

This season began with a remarkable match between two teams from Winnipeg, the Maple Leafs and the Winnipegs, who were trying to qualify for the league. The officers of the league had decided that a five-team league was big enough; they wanted only two Winnipeg teams to join the Kenora, Brandon, and Portage la Prairie teams in the loop, and they already had one Winnipeg team, the Strathconas. The Maple Leafs vs. Winnipegs qualifying game was, according to the *Winnipeg Tribune*, the most brutal hockey match ever witnessed in Manitoba's capital. Several players were injured and the game had to be called before time was up. The man most responsible for the violent play was "Bad" Joe Hall of the Maple Leafs. Hall had learned to play hockey in Brandon. By 1907 he had already established himself as one of professional hockey's tough guys, and he would be involved in skirmish after skirmish until he died, still active in the game, in 1919. In this particular 1907 game he knocked a player named Tobin to the ice. Tobin swung his stick at Hall's legs, but missed. Hall then did something which evidently he was inclined to do throughout his career: he skated back to the man who had angered him and literally whacked him on the head with the stick! Hall was barred from the league for the rest of the year, and he simply packed his bags and travelled to the East to join a professional team in Montreal. But other players in the Manitoba league were capable of playing just as violently as Hall, and several games featured skirmishes, fisticuffs and incidents involving sticks.

Even more distasteful than the players' actions were those of the team owners and operators. By the second week in January the officers of the Kenora and Brandon clubs had decided that their revenues would not meet their expenses. They simply folded their teams and released their players! Then, in February, the owner of the Strathcona Club realized he was going to finish third, so he sold his best and most expensive players to the Maple Leafs. In doing this, he turned down an offer of "financial assistance" from the Portage club that would have enabled him to keep his men — Portage, for its part, wanted to see two mediocre teams in Winnipeg, not one strong one. By late February hockey fans in Manitoba had become disenchanted by the Manitoba professional league, and few of them were disappointed when, early in March, the champions of the league, the Maple Leafs, failed to take the Stanley Cup from the Montreal Wanderers.[14]

This description of the 1907-08 professional hockey season should indicate why J. D. Pratt, C. W. Gordon and other pure amateurs had little trouble supporting their assertions that professional sport was too often a debased form of sport. This was a truth readily acknowledged by virtually everyone. However, a growing number of people were beginning to see that this was not the whole truth. Professional athletes were mercenaries whose performances could be vicious or corrupt, but they were also experts whose skills were superior.

The notion that the professional was an expert as well as a mercenary had been present in Manitoba since the 1870's, and well before that in more developed parts of the world. However, as Frank Cosentino has suggested, it was only around the turn of the century that the professional athlete began to be identified first and foremost as an expert.[15] An athlete, said an anonymous writer in the Winnipeg Saturday Post, becomes a professional "because he is good," and he remains an amateur if he "can't play well enough to get money."[16] The early twentieth century trend was for more and more people to agree with this position.

When one viewed professional sports from the new perspective, one's attitude toward entities such as the MAAA and CAAU changed immensely. The arguments used by officers of these organizations became unconvincing, and their actions seemed rather absurd. They assumed a young man became a professional athlete because he possessed a flawed character and was led into temptation. Perhaps it was more accurate to say that he became a professional because, just like an opera singer or an actor, he had developed his skills to the point where large audiences were willing to pay to watch him display them.[17] The pure amateurs spoke and wrote as if professional athletes were motivated only by money and did not enjoy playing their sport. This seemed implausible, unless one were prepared to argue that doctors, who were well paid for their work, did not enjoy helping the sick to become well.[18] The officers of the MAAA felt it was necessary to professionalize everyone whose acceptance of money was brought to their attention. But could they not have ignored the "violation" by the man who accepted $1.50 for winning a potato race at a country fair?[19] The same officers insisted on professionalizing those who played with and against paid men. But if paid men had a tendency to be violent or to throw games, perhaps they would be discouraged from so doing if they had unpaid teammates.[20] And was it not a bit foolish in any case to make someone into an expert because he associated with experts? The previously-quoted anonymous writer in the *Winnipeg Saturday Post* said he wished the with-or-against clause applied in the newspaper business. If it did, the reporters could become editors by just going to staff picnics.[21]

One must reiterate that the critics of the strict amateur organizations and their philosophy were not saying that the ideas of the pure amateurs were wrong. They were just incomplete. Who were these critics? They were doctors, lawyers, journalists, school teachers, clerks, insurance agents or other private businessmen. Like the pure amateurs, they were members of the "middle" class or "upper" class. The professional versus amateur conflict in Canada can be viewed too easily in "British" terms, as one between "middle" or "upper class" people on the one hand and "lower class" people on the other, with the former supposedly defending pure amateurism and the latter opposing it. The conflict in Manitoba in the early twentieth century was not between members of different classes. The fight against the pure amateurs was led by *rural* people. They were organizers and supporters of the rural clubs in those team sports such as hockey which drew big crowds.

In his new book *Canada Learns to Play*, Alan Metcalfe identifies the low degree of commitment to pure amateurism among early twentieth century rural Canadians.[22] But, he neither elaborates on this, nor explains it. The reason rural Manitobans, at least, opposed strict amateurism becomes reasonably clear if one focusses upon what they wanted changed in the amateur regulations. Essentially, they wanted two alterations. First, players should be allowed to receive money over and above "actual travelling and hotel expenses." This might mean reimbursement for wages lost because work had to be missed, but it could mean simply money accepted to cover the cost of equipment or medical bills. Second, the amateurs should be able to play with and against professionals and not be professionalized for doing so.

Why did rural Manitobans want these changes? Partly because only by having them did it seem that rural Manitoba teams could compete with Winnipeg ones.[23] Over the years they had often felt that Winnipeg clubs were tougher to beat in committee rooms than on the ice or on the playing field. Winnipeg was a big place. There were bound to be reasonably good athletes coming to the city from across the country looking for work or business opportunities. This was not the case in Souris, Neepawa, or even Portage la Prairie or Brandon. Perhaps Winnipeggers supported the MAAA and strict amateurism because relaxed regulations would give rural clubs a better chance to win provincial championships.

However, the main reason rural Manitobans wanted more indulgence of professional practices was because doing so would allow them to see and support higher calibre performances.[24] Rural people were aware, to a degree that Winnipeggers yet were not, that Manitobans could not offer top hockey players the kind of money being offered in eastern Canada, in the northern

United States or, after 1911, in British Columbia. That is the reason some of the greatest hockey players of the era, for example Art Ross, Lester Patrick, "Newsy" Lalonde, and "Cyclone" Taylor, had come to the province but stayed only a short time before moving elsewhere. That is also the reason the best players produced in the province — Joe Hall, Tom Dunderdale, Harry Mummery — would not remain at home. The athletes passing through or leaving Manitoba were the hockey players most capable of delivering the important messages about life that even pure amateurs believed the sport should reveal. Perhaps Manitoba teams should openly pay a few of these players, and round out the teams with unpaid men who would play with and against them.

For the time being too few Winnipeg sportsmen viewed matters in this way. In the 1910's and 1920's, however, the North American professional hockey networks became crystallized, and Manitoba was completely by-passed. At the same time, Manitobans and all Canadians increasingly learned to associate professional sport with excellence as opposed to avarice. This meant that for the people of the keystone province the greatest problem with professional hockey was that they were neither numerous nor wealthy enough to have it. A couple of minor league teams came and went in the 1950s and 1960s, but it was not until the 1970s, by which time the economics of professional hockey were much different than sixty or even twenty years earlier, that Manitobans were able to witness it consistently.

NOTES

1. *Manitoba Free Press* (hereinafter *FP*), March 29, 1911, p. 6.
2. *FP*, April 16, 1904, p. 5, May 7, 1904, p. 7, April 16, 1907, p. 6.
3. See Keith L. Lansley, "The Amateur Athletic Union of Canada and Changing Concepts of Amateurism," Ph.D. thesis, University of Alberta, 1971, pp. 26-63.
4. *FP*, January 15, 1904, p. 5, January 25, 1904, p. 5, January 26, 1904, p. 5.
5. *FP*, April 16, 1907, p. 6.
6. Quoted in Lansley, "The Amateur Athletic Union of Canada," p. 62.
7. On the "war" between the CAAU and the AAF of C, see Don Morrow, "A Case Study in Amateur Conflict: The Athletic War in Canada, 1906-08," *The British Journal of Sports History,* 3 (September, 1986), pp. 173-190.
8. *Hartney Star*, March 22, 1907, p. 4.
9. *Vox Wesleyana*, November 1908, pp. 25-26.
10. *Manitoba College Journal*, March 1910, pp. 18-19.
11. Ralph Connor, *The Prospector, A Tale of the Crow's Nest Pass* (Toronto: Fleming H. Revell Company, 1904), especially chapter 2; Connor, *Corporal Cameron of the North West*

Mounted Police, A Tale of the Macleod Trail (Toronto: The Westminster Co. Ltd., 1912), especially chapter 1.
12. Gordon to *FP,* December 12, 1908, p. 2 of sports section.
13. See the truly remarkable interpretation of ancient history contained in "Live Chat on Sport," *FP,* August 26, 1911, p. 34.
14. The season's developments can be followed through the daily papers in Winnipeg, December 20, 1907-March 13, 1908. On "Bad" Joe Hall, and some of the incidents in which he was involved over the years, see *Winnipeg Tribune,* January 26, 1910, p. 6, *FP,* January 16, 1905, p. 5, April 7, 1919, p. 11, April 8, 1919, p. 10; Stan and Shirley Fischler, *Fischlers' Ice Hockey Encyclopedia,* revised edition (New York: Thomas Y. Cromwell Company, 1979), pp. 242-243.
15. Frank Cosentino, "A History of the Concept of Professionalism in Canadian Sport," Ph.D. thesis, University of Alberta, 1973, especially p. 223.
16. *Winnipeg Saturday Post,* January 25, 1908, p. 7, December 12, 1908, p. 10.
17. *Neepawa Press,* March 11, 1913, p. 2.
18. *Winnipeg Saturday Post,* May 9, 1908, p. 10.
19. *FP,* November 7, 1911, p. 6.
20. *FP,* October 13, 1887, p. 1.
21. *Winnipeg Saturday Post,* May 14, 1910, p. 15. See also *Winnipeg Saturday Post,* January 9, 1909, p. 10 and "Scottie" to *FP,* April 12, 1907, p. 6.
22. Alan Metcalfe, *Canada Learns to Play: The Emergence of Organized Sport, 1807-1914* (Toronto: McClelland and Stewart Ltd., 1987), especially p. 223.
23. *FP,* April 4, 1900, p. 5, November 28, 1905, p. 6, November 29, 1905, p. 7; *Brandon Sun,* December 21, 1911, pt. 1, p. 2., March 7, 1912, pt. 1, p. 7, March 21, 1912, pt. 2, p. 2; *Portage la Prairie Evening Review,* January 6, 1909, p. 8.
24. *FP,* December 3, 1906, p. 6; *Souris Plaindealer,* August 24, 1906, p. 8, November 8, 1906, p. 6, July 12, 1907, p. 8, September 12, 1907, p. 6; *Deloraine Times,* August 8, 1912, p. 4; *Brandon Sun,* December 6, 1906, pt. 1, p. 2, December 21, 1911, pt. 1, p. 2, March 7 1912, pt. 1, p. 7.

BIBLIOGRAPHY AND SUGGESTIONS FOR FURTHER READING

Bailey, Peter. *Leisure and Class in Victorian England: Rational Recreation and the Contest for Control, 1830-1885*. London: Routledge & Kegan Paul, 1978.

Baka, R. A History of Provincial Government Involvement in Sport in Western Canada. Ph.D. Thesis, University of Alberta, 1978.

Blackburn, Cecil. "The Development of Sports in Alberta, 1900-1918." M.A. Thesis, University of Alberta, 1974.

Cosentino, Frank. "A History of the Concept of Professionalism in Canadian Sport." Ph.D. Thesis, University of Alberta, 1973. A History of Canadian Football, 1909-68. M.A. Thesis, University of Alberta, 1969.

Cowie, Isaac. *The Company of Adventurers: A Narrative of Seven Years in the Service of the Hudson's Bay Company During 1867-1874*. Toronto: William Briggs, 1913.

Cox, A. A History of Sports in Canada, 1868-1900. Ph.D. Thesis, University of Alberta, 1969.

Creelman, W. A. *Curling, Past and Present*. Toronto: McClelland and Stewart, 1950.

Culin, Robert Stewart. *Games of the North American Indians*. New York: AMS Press, 1973.

Cunningham, Hugh. *Leisure in the Industrial Revolution c.1780-c.1880*. London: Croom Helm, 1980.

Curtis, E. S. *The North American Indian*. New York: Johnson Reprint Corporation, 1980. (1928).

Eastman, Charles A. *Indian Boyhood*. New York: Dover Publications, 1971.

Ewers, John C. *The Blackfeet*. Norman: University of Oklahoma Press, 1958.

Gorrie, Daniel. *Summers and Winters in the Orkneys*. London: 1865.

Grinnell, George Bird. *The Cheyenne Indians*. Lincoln: University of Nebraska Press, 1972.

Guttman, Allen. *From Ritual to Record: The Nature of Modern Sports*. New York: Columbia University Press, 1978.

Hall, Margaret Ann. "A History of Women's Sport in Canada Prior to World War I." M.A. Thesis, University of Alberta, 1968.

Hallett, W. A History of Federal Government Involvement in the Development of Sport in Canada, 1943-1979. Ph.D. Thesis, University of Alberta, 1981.

Harman, Daniel Williams. *Sixteen Years in the Indian Country: The Journal of Daniel Williams Harman, 1880-1896*. Editor, W. Kaye Lamb. Toronto: Macmillan, 1957.

Howell, Maxwell L. and Howell, Reet. eds. *History of Sport in Canada*. Champaign, Ill.: Stipes Publishing Co. 1981.

Howell, Nancy and Maxwell. *Sports and Games in Canadian Life, 1700 to the Present*. Toronto: Macmillan, 1969.

Isham, James. *James Isham's Observations on Hudson's Bay, 1743*. Toronto: Champlain Society for Hudson Bay Record Society, 1949.

Jobling, I. Sport in Nineteenth Century Canada: The Effects of Technological Changes On Its Development. Ph.D. Thesis, University of Alberta, 1970.

Kane, Paul. *Wanderings of an Artist Among the Indians of North America*. Edmonton: Hurtig Ltd., 1968.

Kerr, John. *History of Curling*. Edinburgh: David Douglas, 1890.

Kroeber, A. L. *Ethnology of the Gros Ventre*. New York: AMS Press, 1978 (1908).

Lansley, Keith L. "The Amateur Athletic Union of Canada and Changing Concepts of Amateurism." Ph.D. Thesis, University of Alberta, 1971.

Lappage, Ronald. "Selected Sports and Canadian Society, 1921-1939." Ph.D. Thesis, University of Alberta, 1974.

Lavine, Sigmund A. *The Games the Indians Played.* New York: Dodd Mead and Company, 1974.

Lund, Rolf. "A History of Skiing in Canada Prior to 1940." M.A. Thesis, University of Alberta, 1971.

Malcolmson, R. W. *Popular Recreations in English Society, 1700-1850.* Cambridge University Press, 1973.

Mangan, J. A. and Park, Roberta J., eds. *From "Fair Sex" to Feminism: Sport and the Socialization of Women in the Industrial and Post-Industrial Eras.* London, Totowa, N. J.: Frank Cass, 1987.

McDougall, John. *Forest Lake and Prairie — Twenty Years of Frontier Life in Western Canada, 1842-62.* Toronto: William Briggs, 1895.

McLennan, W. M. *Sport in Early Calgary.* Calgary: Fort Brisebois Publ., 1983.

Metcalfe, Alan. *Canada Learns to Play: The Emergence of Organized Sport, 1807-1914.* Toronto: McClelland and Stewart Ltd., 1987.

Mitchelson, E. B. "The Evolution of Men's Basketball in Canada, 1892-1936." M.A. Thesis, University of Alberta, 1968.

Morrow, Don, and Keyes, Mary. *A Concise History of Sport in Canada.* Toronto: Oxford University Press, 1989.

Morton, W. L. *The Canadian Identity.* Toronto: University of Toronto Press, 1968.

Mountain Horse, Mike. *My People the Bloods.* Calgary: Glenbow-Alberta Institute, 1979.

Moyles, R. G. (ed). *Challenge of the Homestead, Peace River Letters of Clyde and Myrle Campbell, 1919-1924.* Calgary: Alberta Records Publication Board, Historical Society of Alberta, 1988.

Payne, Michael, "A Social History of York Factory, 1788-1870." Manuscript Report Series, Canadian Parks Service, 1984.

Redmond, Gerald. *The Sporting Scots of Nineteenth-Century Canada.* London and Toronto: Associated University Presses, 1982.

Reid, J. Sports and Games in Alberta Before 1900. M.A. Thesis, University of Alberta, 1969.

Routledge, P. The North-West Mounted Police and Their Influence on the Sporting and Social Life of the North West Territories, 1870-1904. M.A. Thesis, University of Alberta, 1978.

Roxborough, Henry. *One Hundred Not Out: The Story of Nineteenth-Century Canadian Sport.* Toronto, Ryerson Press, 1966.

Sawula, Lorne. *Bibliography of Sources for Canadian History of Sport and Physical Education, 1974.* Collection D796.S271, Glenbow Museum.

Stevenson, John A. *Curling in Ontario, 1846-1946.* Toronto: Ontario Curling Association.

Strange, Kathleen. *With The West in Her Eyes.* Toronto: The Macmillan Company of Canada Ltd., 1945.

Sturrock, D. A History of Rugby Football in Canada. M.A. Thesis, University of Alberta, 1971.

Twin, Stephanie L. ed. Out of the Bleachers: Writings on Women and Sport. Old Westbury, N. Y.: The Feminist Press, 1979.

Vellathottam, T. A History of Lacrosse in Canada Prior to 1914. M.A. Thesis, University of Alberta, 1968.

Voisey, Paul. *Vulcan: The Making of a Prairie Community.* Toronto: University of Toronto Press, 1988.

Wetherell, D. G. and Kmet, I. R. A. *Useful Pleasures: The Shaping of Leisure in Alberta, 1896-1945.* Regina: Alberta Culture and Multiculturalism/Canadian Plains Research Center, forthcoming 1990.

Wise, S. F. and Fisher, Douglas. *Canada's Sporting Heroes.* Don Mills: General Publishing Co., 1974.

Zeman, Brenda. *Hockey Heritage: 88 Years of Puck-Chasing in Saskatchewan.* Regina: WDS Association/Saskatchewan Sports Hall of Fame, 1983.

Zeman, Gary. *Alberta on Ice.* Edmonton: Westweb Press, 1985.

INDEX
(Winter Sports in the West)